PEAK PERFORMANCE TRAINING FOR VOLLEYBALL

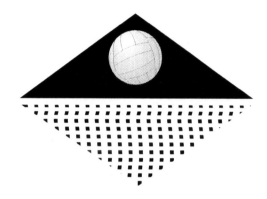

Thomas Emma

COACHES CHOICE™

ISBN: 1-58518-862-X
Library of Congress Control Number: 2003106686
Book layout: Deborah Oldenburg
Illustrations: Judy Picone-Fadeyev
Cover design: Kerry Hartjen
Cover photo: Eugene Garcia/Allsport

Coaches Choice
P.O. Box 1828
Monterey, CA 93942
www.coacheschoice.com

DEDICATION

For my family

ACKNOWLEDGMENTS

I would like to thank the editors and staff at Coaches Choice,
who allow for complete freedom in the writing process,
and especially Bob Brooks for his professionalism and courtesy.

Special thanks to Garret Kirk, who kept on top of me to finish the manuscript,
and to Judy Picone-Fadeyev, Creative Director of The DaVinci Corporation,
for her hard work and timeliness with the illustrations.
Thanks to Chris Muller of Muller Media Conversions, Inc.
for his computer expertise. And of course, to Marie
for keeping the shop running while I worked on this project.

And finally, thanks to all the hard-working volleyball players and coaches
who make improvement a way of life. Good luck to all.

CONTENTS

INTRODUCTION

No one would argue that the game of volleyball is more competitive than ever before in its history. Popularity and participation at all levels of play have risen many-fold in recent years, bringing about fierce competition for roster spots, playing time, college scholarships, and team victories. To be successful in the current climate, volleyball players understand that they must do everything humanly possible to reach their full potential.

Because of this ever present and formidable competition throughout the volleyball universe, concepts such as strength, conditioning, and athletic enhancement training have come to the forefront. No longer is jogging a couple of miles per day and pumping out a few push-ups periodically in the off-season sufficient for volleyball players. Athletes must train rigorously year-round, and come the first day of preseason practice, nothing less than top physical condition is expected. Today's coaches demand this of their players, and not showing up in shape is a sure ticket to riding the bench when the regular season begins.

Okay, now that you know how important being in top-flight condition is to success on the volleyball court, how do you go about achieving it? A good start is right here in your hands. *Peak Performance Training for Volleyball* is your road map toward optimum volleyball shape. It presents a comprehensive and easy to understand blueprint that you and your coaches can follow on a year-round basis. Of course, reading and studying the book is not enough. It is up to you to put in the consistent effort and work. But combining the precise instruction that the book provides with your determination and enthusiasm can only yield one result: a better all-around volleyball player.

Peak Performance Training for Volleyball is divided into four sections. Part One features strategies that will help you to maintain peak performance levels. The topics include warm-up, cool-down, flexibility, recuperation, sleep, overtraining, injury prevention and rehabilitation, along with an entire chapter on volleyball nutrition, which includes information on the controversial subject of food supplements.

Part Two deals exclusively with volleyball conditioning. It begins with the basics (energy systems and general volleyball fitness guidelines) and continues with detailed explanations of aerobic and anaerobic conditioning. Comprehensive sample aerobic and anaerobic training programs are also included.

Part Three covers all aspects of strength training as it relates to volleyball, including strength-training basics and principles, core-training protocol, and exercise execution explanations and their corresponding illustrations. A year-round strength-training program, complete with sample routines for each of six training cycles, is detailed at the end of the section.

Part Four introduces you to movement training for volleyball. This section provides thorough descriptions of various techniques and drills that will help you improve your balance, speed, quickness, and jumping ability.

A Special Note to Readers

The exercises and drills explained and illustrated in this book follow carefully planned guidelines. By using the information as presented, you will experience the best possible results. As with all exercise programs, be sure to see your physician before you begin.

PART I
KEYS TO MAINTAINING PEAK PERFORMANCE

CHAPTER 1

Warm-Up, Cool-Down, and Flexibility

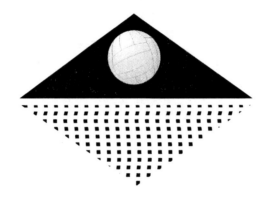

Without question the two most neglected aspects of sports conditioning are the *warm-up and cool-down*. Unfortunately, many athletes, especially young athletes, in their haste to get to the main task at hand (conditioning/strength workout, practice, match, etc.), rush through or forsake altogether the warm-up process. Just as commonplace are athletes who forego the post-workout cool-down— a warm shower and a bite to eat certainly sounds more appealing than cooling down on a stationary bike and hitting the floor for more stretching.

The temptation of bypassing warm-up and cool-down activities is certainly understandable. After all, these disciplines are in a word: boring. They are, however, *essential* components of balanced conditioning, and all volleyball players, regardless of age or level, must take them seriously. The risks of not engaging in a thorough warm-up and cool-down are numerous and include falling short of your athletic potential and sustaining injury. Enough said.

Warm-Up

Warming up prior to any type of intense physical activity be it a match, workout, or practice is a three-fold process, which includes *light exertion* for five to eight minutes, followed by a *comprehensive stretching routine* like the one detailed later in this chapter, and finishing with *low-intensity involvement* in the desired activity. Warming up correctly will contribute to productive workouts, enhanced performance in-between the lines, and most important, the prevention of injuries.

Cool-Down

The equally important cool-down consists of a few minutes *low-intensity activity* similar to the first step of the warm-up process, followed by an abbreviated *flexibility session* that focuses on the lower back, hamstrings, and shoulder region. Actively cooling down after high- intensity exertion of any kind will help the body recover, along with allowing it to return to its relaxed state faster, thus promoting physiological balance and sound sleep. All competitive volleyball players know how difficult it is to wind down and fall asleep after an intense evening match. Cooling down in the manner described will alleviate this problem to some extent. An example of the warm-up/cool-down continuum is detailed in Table 1-1.

Warm-Up Phase 1–Low-Intensity Activity
Perform five to eight minutes of light exercise, such as running in place, stationary biking, or slow-paced jogging. This type of activity raises your body temperature and gets the blood flowing to your muscles, which will allow you to stretch (phase 2) through a greater range of motion.

Prepares the body for

Warm-Up Phase 2–Flexibility Training
12 stretches (detailed in the next section)

Prepares the body for

Warm-Up Phase 3–Medium-Intensity Involvement in Desired Activity
Examples: Strength training—two light, high repetition (15 to 20) sets
Plyometric training—low-intensity bounding
Agility training—jumping rope at medium speed

Prepares the body for

Intense All-Out Activity

Cool-Down Phase 1–Low-Intensity Activity (See Warm-Up Phase 1)
Cool-Down Phase 2–Abbreviated Flexibility Routine
Six to eight stretches with an emphasis on the lower back, hamstrings, and shoulders.

Table 1-1. Warm-up/cool-down continuum

Flexibility Training

Arrive at any major sporting event an hour or so early and what you're likely to witness are numerous athletes spread over the floor, field, or track in various states of contortion. Likewise, linger around after that same high-level athletic contest, and a similar scene will be taking place. What they are doing of course is *stretching*, preparing their bodies for competition on one end of the spectrum and cooling themselves down on the other.

The previous examples just underscore how *flexibility training* has come of age throughout the sports world. Every competitive (and non-competitive) athlete must make a priority of improving and maintaining flexibility. Volleyball players are certainly no exception to this important rule. Regular stretching will make you less susceptible to injury, enhance recovery, and improve speed, agility, and explosive power. Flexibility work should be religiously performed both before and after your conditioning workouts. Stretching before workouts readies the body for strenuous exercise. Post-workout stretching is essential for recovery, as it assists in the removal of lactic acid (lactate), a substance that contributes to muscle soreness. Less flexible athletes may want to include some extra stretching before breakfast in the morning and prior to retiring at night.

Flexibility training requires *full concentration*. As each stretch is executed, be sure to maintain awareness of how the muscle feels. Work to the point of slight discomfort but never to the point of pain. Injured athletes must take great care to follow this advice or risk aggravating the injury. As previously discussed, it is advisable to do some light exercise for five to eight minutes prior to pre-workout flexibility training. This will loosen your muscles and joints and allow you to stretch more fully. Each individual stretch should be held for 20 to 50 seconds. This method of holding a stretch is called *static stretching* and is much safer than ballistic stretching where bouncing movements are used. Ballistic stretching has made somewhat of a resurgence in sports-conditioning circles in recent years with many strength and conditioning coaches prescribing it to their athletes. However, the risk of injury is just too high with this type of flexibility training, and therefore all volleyball players should avoid it.

Before ending this section, two popular modes of flexibility training used by many professional and elite college athletes should be covered. The first, *passive partner stretching*, entails having a partner add light pressure to each stretch to increase joint and muscle range of motion. The other is known as *proprioceptive neuromuscular facilitation (PNF) stretching*, and involves a partner/facilitator leading an athlete through a series of positions (contract, hold, relax, and movement) in 10-second intervals. Both techniques have benefits if performed correctly and with the appropriate assisting personnel. Unfortunately, the majority of junior high school and high school athletic departments, along with many smaller college programs, do not have individuals on staff who are capable of teaching these techniques correctly and safely.

Incorrect execution of these methods can lead to injury. In light of this, players should incorporate static stretching exclusively in their flexibility programs unless knowledgeable assisting personnel are available on a regular basis.

Flexibility Program

The following *flexibility program* details a stretching regime that is appropriate for volleyball players. The entire routine can be accomplished in 10 to 15 minutes. It should be performed on a year-round basis even during training breaks. As you progress and become more flexible, feel free to add and subtract stretches as you see fit.

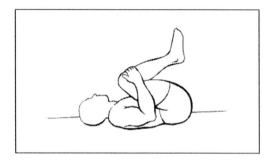 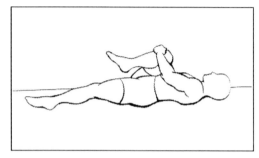

1. Knees to Chest

- Lie flat on your back with your legs extended.
- Grasp your upper shins just below your kneecaps and pull your knees to your chest. Hold for 30 seconds.
- Alternate by pulling one leg at a time while keeping the other leg extended on the floor. Hold for 30 seconds.
- Perform two sets—one set with both legs and one set with alternating legs.

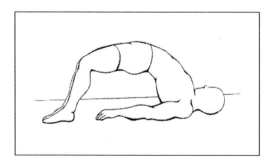

2. Back Arch

- Lie flat on your back with your legs extended.

- Flex your knees, sliding your feet toward your buttocks, and lift your pelvis off the floor, while arching your back.
- Perform one set. Hold in an arched position for 45 to 60 seconds.

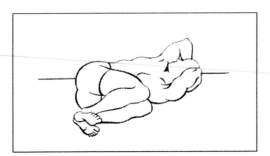

3. Hip Flexor Stretch

- Lie flat on your back with your knees flexed and your hands clasped behind your neck.
- Slowly lower both knees simultaneously to the floor, keeping your head, shoulders, and elbows flat on the floor. Hold at the bottom for 20 seconds.
- Perform two sets for each side.

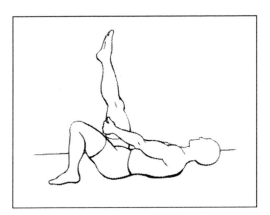

4. Lying Hamstring Stretch

- Lie flat on your back with your legs flexed and your heels close to the buttocks.
- Extend one leg upward and grasp underneath it. Then slowly pull it toward you while keeping the other leg as straight as possible. Hold for 30 seconds.
- Perform two sets with each leg.

5. Reverse Plough

- Lie face down on the floor with your body extended.
- Place your palms on the floor between your chest and your hips.
- Press down evenly, and raise your head and trunk straight upward. Hold for 30 seconds.
- Perform two sets.

 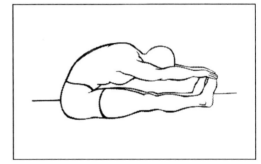

6. Plough to Hamstring Stretch.

- Lie flat on your back with your arms on your hips.
- Raise both slightly bent legs up over your head and slowly lower your feet to the floor.
- After holding the stretch for 30 seconds, return under control to the seated position with your legs extended in front of you.
- Keeping both legs straight, bend forward at the waist and lower your trunk to your thighs, while simultaneously stretching your hands to your toes. Hold for 30 seconds.
- Perform two sets.

7. Back/Quadriceps Stretch

- Lie face down on the floor with your body extended.

- Reach back and grab both ankles.

- Pull your ankles toward your upper back while at the same time lifting your chest off the floor.

- Perform one set. Hold for 45 seconds.

8. Standing Groin Stretch

- Stand with your legs spread approximately twice as wide as your shoulders.

- Bend straight down and attempt to touch your hands to the floor. Hold for 20 seconds.

- Perform two sets.

9. Standing Quadriceps Stretch.

- Stand upright bracing yourself with one hand against a wall for balance.
- Reach down and grasp one foot (right hand/right foot; left hand/left foot).
- Pull your heel to your buttocks and hold for 20 seconds.
- Perform two sets with each leg.

10. Calf Stretch

- Stand upright with both hands against a wall and your arms fully extended.
- Lean forward with your feet remaining flat on the floor, bending your arms and stretching your calves. Hold for 30 seconds.
- Perform two sets.

 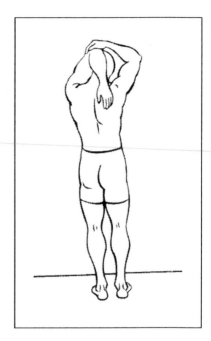

11. Shoulder Stretch

- Stand upright and cross one wrist over the other and interlock your hands.
- With your arms extended behind your head, shrug your shoulders upwards and reach toward the ceiling. Hold for 30 seconds.
- Perform one set with your hands clasped each way.

12. Triceps Stretch

- Sit or stand with one arm flexed and raised overhead next to your ear; rest your hand on your shoulder blade.
- Grasp your elbow with the opposite hand and pull it behind your head. Hold for 20 seconds.
- Perform two sets with each arm.

Pre-Movement Training Exercises

Prior to all movement-training workouts (plyometric, agility, speed, non-machine assisted anaerobic training, etc.) you should perform the following series of exercises. These low- to medium-intensity movements will set the stage for high-intensity training. When appropriate, pre-movement training exercises will follow your conventional warm-up covered earlier in this chapter.

Exercise: Leg Swings

Execution: Stand sideways to a wall and brace yourself against it with your inside hand. With your outside hand at your side and your outside leg planted firmly on the ground, swing your inside leg straight in front of your body and then back behind your body.

Sets and Repetitions: Two sets of 15 repetitions with each leg.

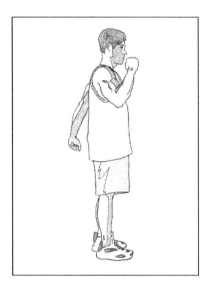

Exercise: Arm Swings

Execution: Stand with your knees slightly bent and your legs shoulder-width apart and repetitively swing your arms forward and back as if you were sprinting.

Sets and Repetitions: Two sets of 20 repetitions.

Exercise: Knee-Ups

Execution: Standing with a straight posture, attempt to lift one knee as high as possible while keeping the other leg planted firmly on the ground. Your arms can either hang at your sides or swing up and down as if you were running in place.

Sets and Repetitions: Two sets of 15 repetitions for each leg.

Exercise: Side Kick

Execution: Stand facing a wall and brace both of your slightly bent arms against it. You will be two to three feet away from the wall depending on your height and the length of your arms. Proceed, with your knee flexed slightly, to swing your leg from side to side, while keeping your other leg planted firmly on the ground.

Sets and Repetitions: Two sets of 15 repetitions with each leg.

Exercise: Butt Kicks

Execution: Run straight ahead at an easy pace attempting to kick your heels toward your buttocks.

Sets and Repetitions: Two sets of 20 to 25 yards.

Exercise: Body-Weight Side Lunge

Execution: Standing straight with your hands at your sides or clasped behind your head, step to the side, bend at the knees, and bring your back knee close to the floor. Proceed to drive yourself under control back to the standing position.

Sets and Repetitions: Two sets of 15 repetitions for each leg.

Exercise: Carioca

Execution: Begin in an athletic stance—head up, back straight, legs spread slightly wider than shoulder-width, and knees flexed. Proceed to step to the side with your left foot, followed by stepping behind your left foot with your right foot, simultaneously turning your hips in the direction you want to go. Then push your right leg powerfully in front of your left leg and continue in that pattern for the required distance. Change direction and repeat.

Sets and Repetitions: Two sets of 20 yards in each direction.

CHAPTER 2

Recuperation, Overtraining, and Injuries

If volleyball players hope to perform at peak levels of efficiency on a year-round basis, they must take adequate time to recover between exercises, workouts, and training cycles, get sufficient amounts of sound sleep and rest, avoid overtraining, and deal conscientiously with injuries. The following are a few ways to achieve these objectives.

Recuperation

If you are to progress toward peak levels of performance, you must give your body adequate opportunity to *recover*. This not only means recovery time between exercises or drills within a workout, but between the workouts and training cycles as well. Recuperation requires a very individual and delicate *balance*. No two athletes have the exact same recovery needs. Some players are able to recover very quickly from even the most strenuous of training sessions, while others get the most out of their training programs by employing maximum rest intervals. It is up to you to become accustomed to your individual need for recovery and act accordingly.

With experience, you'll begin develop an *intuitive feel* for when to push ahead with intense training, and when to take a step back. Especially important for volleyball players is the ability to monitor how their legs are responding to various forms of training (strength work, plyometrics, running, etc.). Legs are an explosive athlete's essence, and heavy, tired wheels can wreak havoc on volleyball performance. An approach coaches can use with volleyball athletes is to encourage them to take inventory on how their legs feel and how they recover after training at different intensities during the off-season, and then translate that knowledge to the season when it counts. This strategy gives them a realistic indication of how much their bodies can tolerate in terms of leg training. Remember, too much training can be just as debilitating to performance as too little.

Sleep

Coaches should always tell their athletes, "If you want to soar with the eagles in the daytime, you can't hoot with the owls at night." This is sound advice. As a hard-training athlete, you must get *adequate sleep and rest*. Sleep requirements vary from person to person. Some people are able to get by on only five or six hours per night with no ill effects. While others need up to 10 hours every night to be at their best. Most active volleyball players will require seven-and-a-half to eight hours of sound sleep per night. Younger athletes (i.e., 13 to 18 years old) will usually need more sleep than their older counterparts. Short naps (20 to 30 minutes) can help to rejuvenate you and are suggested if you have the time and inclination. Longer naps (2 to 3 hours) tend to cause grogginess and should be avoided, especially on the day of a match.

Coffee and other highly caffeinated drinks (certain colas, tea, etc.) should be kept to a minimum, especially late in the day, as these products can contribute to insomnia. Also, exercising vigorously later at night can make it difficult to fall asleep. (You all know how hard it is to sleep after participating in an intense night match). Warm milk and soft cheeses consumed close to bedtime can sometimes improve the quality of your sleep, as can taking a warm bath two to three hours prior to retiring.

As with training, your body will usually tell you how much sleep you need on a daily basis. Just make sure that you take the time to listen.

Overtraining

Being in an overtrained state is the *enemy* of any athlete. It retards progress, inhibits performance, and can lead to injury. As a volleyball player engaging in a full slate of conditioning disciplines, you must remain acutely aware of how your body is responding to the stresses of intense physical activity. If you don't, overtraining is sure to occur.

You'll find both good news and bad news on the overtraining front. First, the bad news: no one has ever achieved the perfect balance between training and rest. The good news, however, is that by following the principles detailed in this book, you're chances of becoming overtrained are slim. The following points provide a list of common symptoms of overtraining, as well as some proven remedies if your body does become overtrained.

Symptoms

- Noticeable loss of strength, power, and conditioning
- Increased muscle, joint, and tendon soreness
- Lack of enthusiasm for training
- A preponderance of minor injuries
- Insomnia

Remedies

- Take a break from training (one to two weeks).
- Decrease intensity of workouts.
- Change up your routine.
- Include some extra stretching and warm-up/cool-down activities in your workouts.

If possible, analyze your training for a month or so prior to when you began to feel the effects of overtraining. This step will help you to pinpoint possible problems and how to avoid them in the future.

Injury Prevention

Injury *prevention* is a key to a long and successful athletic career. Volleyball players, because of the nature of their sport, are prone to many impact and overuse-related injuries. Some of the most common injuries include sprained ankles, lower back strains, shin splints, and a variety knee and shoulder ailments. Fortunately you can curtail the incidence of these and other injuries. The secret: *condition your body to its fullest potential*.

By following the training programs and suggestions in *Peak Performance Training for Volleyball*, you can greatly reduce your risk of injury. Warming up and cooling down properly, improving flexibility, and adhering to a balanced nutritional plan (one that helps you achieve your optimal body weight) all contribute substantially to preventing injury.

Of all conditioning disciplines, *strength training* is perhaps the most integral component when it comes to the prevention of injury. The additional strength and lean muscle tissue you build around your joints, especially the joints of the shoulders and knees, act as a shock absorber during high-impact activity such as landing after a block or spike, and as a stress reducer during overuse activities (i.e., repetitive shoulder swings.) A strong lower back and mid-section stave off a variety of lower back problems, including a frustrating condition called *sciatica*, which gives rise to pain extending from the lower back to the lower leg and foot. Anyone who has experienced this injury knows how important prevention is, because once sciatica occurs it can become chronic and long lasting, not to mention extremely painful.

Finally, always maintain an awareness of your body and how it feels from day to day, especially during the long, grueling volleyball season. Minor aches and pains can oftentimes be precursors to full-blown injuries. Recognizing these kinks and acting accordingly (extra rest, special treatment, additional warm-up, etc.) can help you avoid many injuries before they manifest.

In today's competitive world of volleyball, remaining *healthy* and at full strength for extended periods of time can mean the difference between success and failure for both players and teams. Those athletes who condition themselves optimally have the best chance of playing peak performance volleyball week after week, month after month, and year after year without injury getting in the way.

A Special Note for Young Female Volleyball Players

While all volleyball players, regardless of age or gender, should train their lower bodies hard in the weight room, young female athletes have an added incentive. Studies have shown that those young women who participate in movement-oriented sports such as basketball, soccer, and volleyball are as much as eight times more likely than their male counterparts to tear the anterior cruciate ligament (ACL) in the knee. Although numerous theories exist as to why, it seems women have looser ligaments and an imbalance in strength between their quadriceps (stronger) and hamstrings (weaker). To counteract this condition and lesson the chance of sustaining an ACL injury, which, by the way, can keep you on the shelf for the better part of a year, women volleyball players should emphasize exercises that build the hamstrings and protect the knee area such as deep squats, straight-legged dead lifts, and hamstring curls in their training.

Injury Rehabilitation

Despite the high level of conditioning most volleyball players attain today, injuries are still an inevitable part of the game. The constant jumping, quick movements, and dives to the floor that volleyball requires make it virtually impossible for even the most gifted and conscientious athletes to escape injury forever. Because of this reality, the remainder of this chapter includes some injury *rehabilitation tips* that should make your journey from injury back to the court at little easier. Keep in mind that this information is not meant to take the place of consulting and working closely with experienced medical and rehabilitation personnel.

- *Let them know*: When you first sustain an injury of any kind—whether it is a sprained ankle, twisted knee, or hyper-extended elbow—the first step is to communicate with the appropriate individuals (trainers, doctors, coaches, etc.). A clear and succinct explanation of your injury is crucial for proper diagnosis and a key to quick recovery. Doctors and trainers, while experienced in dealing with injured athletes, are not mind readers. Being as precise as possible when describing your injury will go a long way toward ensuring that the suitable treatment/rehabilitation protocol will be prescribed.

- *Choose the right physical therapist*: Once a doctor has examined you, it is time to go about the process of choosing a physical therapist to help you rehabilitate. While most college programs have trained rehabilitation personnel on staff, the large majority of high schools and junior high schools do not. Therefore it may very well be up to you and your family to choose a physical therapist.

  First, you should *seek recommendations*, particularly from those individuals who've experienced a similar injury and followed it up with a successful rehabilitation. Your coaches and athletic trainers may be able to provide you with physical therapist recommendations as well.

  Second, after you've narrowed down the field of therapist candidates to two or three, *go visit each of them*. This will allow you to get a feel for the therapist, while at the same time assessing the facilities. When evaluating the facilities, pay particular attention to the atmosphere, since rehabilitation workouts will take all the enthusiasm you can muster.

  Finally, once you make the choice, *stick with it.* Switching physical therapists in midstream will cause a major disruption and hinder your progress.

- *Be consistent*: Consistency is an essential factor in any progressive strength and conditioning program. Injury rehabilitation training is no different. Missing treatment and/or rehab sessions even periodically is not an option for the competitive volleyball player. If your goal is to get back to the court at full strength as soon as possible, adhering to a consistent rehabilitation schedule is a must. Remember, *consistency plus hard work equals a successful rehabilitation.*

- *Patience*: Your patience will be severely tested when coming back from an injury. During the rehabilitation process, patience is not only a virtue but a necessity. Like it or not (and you probably won't), the body has its own timetable for recovery independent of your opinion about it. It only responds to the proper ratio of exercise, treatment, and rest spread over the appropriate period of time. Realizing this need for patience early on will save you much anguish and frustration.

- *Don't come back too soon*: Although you will surely be tempted (all dedicated athletes are), coming back to action after an injury before you're ready is a major mistake, one that will put you at a high risk of re-injury, not to mention the high probability for a lackluster performance. The list of high-profile athletes who return too soon from injury only to re-injure themselves would fill this book many times over. Regardless of the outside pressures you may experience from coaches, teammates, and family members, make sure to take all the time you need for *recovery and rehabilitation* before jumping back into the competitive fray. In the long run this approach will be best for both you and your team.

CHAPTER 3

Volleyball Nutrition

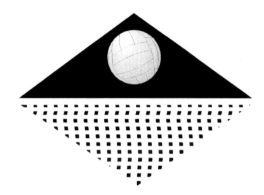

Nutrition has become quite a complicated and contentious subject in recent years. In fact, it has turned into a virtual battleground, where opinions, claims, and suggestions run the proverbial gamut. Foods that where once considered nutritious and healthy are today, according to some, to be avoided at all cost. Other foods, which up until recently were said to cause a myriad of serious health problems, currently stand as the darlings of the nutritional world.

What is a volleyball player to make of all this? And, more to the point, how should a hard-training volleyball athlete plan a peak performance nutritional program? The advice in this book is simple and is limited to two words, the same two words your coaches drill into your head day in and day out on the practice floor: *stay balanced*. A balanced diet, complete with ample complex carbohydrates, reasonable amounts of high-quality protein, adequate fat intake, and plenty of water, is still the ticket for high performance in the competitive world of sports.

Components of Balanced Nutrition

Water

Approximately two-thirds of your body mass is composed of *water*. It is without question the most important ingredient in any athlete's diet. Water performs many functions in the body, including lubricating joints, modulating body temperature (a key factor during vigorous exercise), carrying nutrients to cells and waste products away from cells, and helping the digestion and absorption of food.

It is imperative that you drink a minimum of eight 12-ounce glasses of water each day. On hot humid days, or when high levels of energy are expended such as during two-a-day preseason workouts, up to 12 glasses should be consumed. Other liquids such as lemonade, various fruit juices, and sports drinks basically have the same effect on the body as pure water. (All are water based.) Pure water is still the simplest (and cheapest) way to stay hydrated, however. Alcoholic, caffeinated, and carbonated drinks should be avoided, as they contain ingredients that actually dehydrate the body. Always make sure to keep your fluid intake high before, during, and after exercise sessions, as well as consistent throughout the day. Remaining optimally hydrated on a daily basis contributes to buoyant health and peak athletic performance. Make it a part of your lifestyle.

Carbohydrates (% of total calories = 55% to 60%. Calories per gram= 4)

Carbohydrates are the easiest form of food for the body to turn into *energy*. They are, however, not all created equal. *Complex carbohydrates*—which include rice, potatoes, vegetables, beans, breads, and pastas—provide long-term energy and are easily digested. These foods contain necessary nutrients such as B vitamins and should be the mainstays of a volleyball player's meal plan. Complex carbohydrates will always be the primary part of your pre-match or pre-workout meal. *Simple carbohydrates*, such as fruits and processed sugars, while easily digested, provide only short-term energy. With the exception of fresh fruit and fruit juices, which provide excellent sources of important nutrients (minerals, fiber, vitamins) and do not rapidly lower blood sugar levels, simple carbohydrates should be eaten only in moderation.

How many grams of carbohydrates should you consume per day? It depends on your activity level. As a rule of thumb, when engaging in heavy training multiply your body weight by five to derive the appropriate number of carbohydrate grams to be consumed each day. During light training times or over workout breaks use three as the multiplier. Of course these are just approximations and much depends on the speed of your individual metabolism. As with your training, it is best to get a feel through trial and error for how your body responds to different amounts of food and act accordingly.

Proteins (% of total calories = 25% to 30%. Calories per gram = 4)

Protein is used by the body to *build and repair* muscle tissue. Obviously, hard-training volleyball players who are engaging in demanding activities such as weightlifting and plyometric training should include ample amounts of protein in their diets. The best sources of protein are eggs, fish, red meat, poultry, and diary products. These foods are referred to as *complete proteins*, since they contain all the amino acids necessary to build muscle. *Incomplete proteins*, such as most plant proteins, lack one or more of the essential amino acids and can only contribute to the muscle building process if consumed in the proper combinations. Unless you are involved in a weight-gaining program (see later in this section), eating approximately .50 to .60 grams of protein daily per pound of body weight should be sufficient for a volleyball player.

Fats (% of total calories = 15% to 20%. Calories per gram = 9)

Fats, similar to proteins and carbohydrates, are needed by the body. They supply the body with a major source of energy, protect vital organs, and help to prevent starvation during times of insufficient food intake. The problem is that the average American, including many athletes, derives up to 50 percent of his calories from fat. While the once popular extremely low- fat diet is not suggested here, neither is the 50-percent fat diet. This amount of fat consumption can add unwanted weight to the physique and raise cholesterol levels, which increases the risk of heart disease. Make a conscious effort to stay away from fried foods, fatty meats, and high-fat diary products. To keep your fat intake *reasonable*, you should try to get the majority of your protein from low-fat sources, such as fish, egg whites, skim or 1% fat milk, lean red meats, and poultry.

Vitamins

Vitamins perform a variety of important functions. For example, vitamin D assists in the absorption of calcium and vitamin C enhances resistance to infection. While vitamins are not a source of energy, they do release energy from the food you eat. Vitamins are only needed by the body in small amounts and can be obtained from eating a balanced, nutritionally sound diet with limited supplementation.

Two types of vitamin classifications exist: *water-soluble* (B and C) and *fat-soluble* (A, D, E, and K). Water-soluble vitamins are not stored in the body. Thus, extra amounts are flushed from the system easily. On the other hand, fat-soluble vitamins are stored in the body's fat and can be toxic if excessive amounts are ingested.

Minerals

More than 20 mineral elements are found in the body, 17 of which are necessary in your diet. Some of the most *important minerals* include calcium, copper, iodine, iron, magnesium, manganese, phosphorus, potassium, and zinc. Minerals help build strong bones, maintain bodily tissues, and help muscles work efficiently. Most minerals that your body requires can be obtained by eating a balanced diet.

Nutritional Supplements

The vast array of nutritional supplements available today is mind-boggling. Some promise to build massive amounts of strength and muscle. Others claim to burn fat, making bodies lean and muscularly defined. Still others, like creatine, are said to improve sports and workout performance.

Regardless of whether you personally believe the previous claims or not, one thing is not debatable: nutritional supplements are big business. Sales are estimated at $50 million annually and growing. Many of the dollars are spent by young athletes looking for that elusive competitive edge. The major reason for the popularity of nutritional supplements, other than the brilliant marketing efforts by the supplement manufacturers, is their well-documented use by superstar athletes. A prominent example is Barry Bonds, debatably major league baseball's all-time greatest ballplayer, who credits some of his success on the field and in the weight room to the use of these products.

Despite their widespread use and popularity, the jury is still out as to how much benefit dietary supplements actually provide. Many nutritional experts believe that if you're eating a well-balanced, nutritionally complete diet, your need for supplementation is minimal. Taking a daily multi-vitamin is fine, as is snacking on an energy bar prior to a workout, but the other stuff, such as protein powders, so-called mega-mass tablets, and fat-burning pills and drinks, are mostly a waste of money, and are more likely to produce stomach cramps and insomnia than they are to improve sports performance. In fact, an extra helping of egg whites and little less late night pizza will help build muscle and reduce fat much more effectively than the majority of these expensive, well-promoted supplements.

Before ending this section, you should be aware of two popular dietary supplements. The first, *glucosamine chondroitin*, has shown to substantially lesson joint soreness, particularly in the knee and shoulder regions, two extremely important areas of the body for volleyball players. This product is highly touted throughout Europe, and while the United States medical community has been slower to endorse it, there appears to be no harmful side affects.

Experimenting with glucosamine chondroitin, especially for those volleyball players recovering from any type of joint injury/surgery, is probably a good idea. The dosage recommendations vary somewhat, but two to three pills per day containing a combination of 1500 mg. of glucosamine and 1200 mg. of chondroitin should be sufficient. This product is widely available at drugs stores and nutritional supplement stores.

The second popular supplement, *creatine*, seems to have performance-enhancing merit. It is a natural substance manufactured in the body, and serves as a small energy source, assisting in the performance of explosive, short-duration movements such as jumping and intense weightlifting. According to proponents, adding or *loading* creatine into the system will enhance an athlete's ability to execute explosive actions. Be aware that creatine supplementation does not actually build muscle; it allows you to work out harder, with the byproduct being more strength and muscle development.

The rate at which creatine is generated in the body is approximately two grams per day. Recommended supplementation guidelines calls for four to six grams daily for five days (loading phase), followed by two grams per day thereafter (maintenance phase). Creatine usually comes in powdered form and should be mixed with water or fruit juice for ingestion.

If you do decide to supplement your diet with creatine it is imperative that you *consume extra water*. This may help limit cramping, which is a common complaint among regular creatine users. Keep in mind that while creatine has been researched more than most nutritional supplements, many professionals in the medical community still feel more study needs to be done on the long-term effects of creatine use. Before engaging in a creatine supplementation program you should consult your physician.

Steroids and Other Performance-Enhancing Drugs

First of all, it is important to note that under no circumstances should a volleyball player, or any athlete for that matter, engage in the use of anabolic steroids or other so-called performance enhancing drugs, regardless of the tremendous amount of pressure exerted on them to excel.

Players at all levels seem to be getting bigger, stronger, and faster every year. As mentioned in the introduction to this book, the competition is fierce for roster spots, playing time, and team wins. Because of this, players may be tempted to experiment with these performance-enhancing drugs such as steroids—but they should not do so.

Adding to the problem (and the confusion) is the availability of legal steroid precursors such as androstenedione (popularly known as andro) that are sold over the counter at health food stores. These derivatives are metabolized into steroids once they enter the body, and according to many in the medical community, have the same dangerous side effects as steroids. Hopefully, steroid precursors will be added to the illegal list soon (Congress is working on it), but at this time they give the wrong impression of being harmless. They're not!

Perhaps the most disconcerting aspect concerning performance-enhancing substances is there popularity among youngsters. Reports have children as young as 10 experimenting with these dangerous drugs, and according to the latest national survey done for federal drug agencies, nearly 500,000 teenagers in the United States use steroids to some degree each year. And that estimate may be substantially low, as most steroid abusers are extremely careful to keep their use hidden. Add to this the aforementioned burgeoning market for steroid precursors and there may be a full-fledged epidemic developing. Coaches, trainers, and most importantly, parents should do everything in their power to discourage youngsters from using these dangerous products. The following are just some of the dangerous side effects of using steroids:

- Liver cancer
- High blood pressure
- Increased risk of heart disease
- Impaired immune system

- Muscle pulls and tears
- Joint problems
- Irritability
- Excessive aggressiveness

Alcohol, Recreational Drugs, and Tobacco

For a serious, hard-training athlete, *staying clear* of alcohol, drugs, and tobacco should be obvious. Unfortunately, in our complicated society, fraught with hard choices and peer pressure, it is not always so cut and dry. However, a few things are certain and can't be debated: using any of these substances, even on a casual basis, can lead to addiction, serious health problems, and a reduction in athletic performance. Numerous well-known athletes from a variety of sports have short-circuited their careers due to their use and abuse of these products. So, do yourself and your game a favor, abstain from alcohol, drugs, and tobacco.

Weight Control

Volleyball players have a variety of reasons for wanting to *gain or lose weight*. Some may need to increase their physical strength and power for spiking and blocking, thus requiring some added muscular body weight. Others desire to lose weight to increase their speed, quickness, and stamina. In either case, athletes should be sure to work within their genetic make-up and body type (i.e., *ectomorph*: slim build; *mesomorph*: muscular build; *endomorph*: heavy/large build, etc.) and aspire to maintain a reasonably low-level of body-fat—6 to 12 percent for men and 12 to 18 percent for women. The next part of this chapter reviews several simple strategies for gaining or losing weight.

Weight Gain

To gain weight in a safe and efficient manner, you should focus on two major factors. First, you must *take in more calories* than you expend—not always easy for the hard-training volleyball player. Second, you should engage in a year-round *strength training program* that focuses on building maximum muscle mass by incorporating basic multi-joint exercises (see Part III for strength training explanations) for low to medium repetition sets (4 to 10 reps). This approach will ensure that the weight you gain comes in the form of lean muscle mass and not unwanted fat.

Always keep in mind that being in weight-gaining mode doesn't mean you have open clearance to eat anything and everything you want. Your fat consumption should remain relatively low, and overstuffing yourself with starchy carbohydrates is strongly discouraged. Gaining large amounts of body fat will inhibit performance and can eventually cause health problems. Small amounts of extra protein can and should be added to your diet during a weight-gain cycle, but take care not to overdo it, as do many well-intentioned young athletes who gorge themselves with protein in futile attempts to pack on muscle. The fact is that the body can only effectively metabolize 30 to 35 grams of protein (approximately one-and-a-half cans of tuna) at a given time. The best way to get maximum protein into your diet is to incorporate five or six small meals spread three-to-four hours apart over the course of a day. Weight gaining programs, in most cases, should be undertaken during the off-season.

Weight Loss

For volleyball players who wish to lose weight, the first point to be aware of is that the scale should never be the ultimate judge. The most important factor in sound weight management is *body composition* (relative amounts of muscle, bone, and fat in the body). Overweight athletes should always make losing fat and gaining lean muscle tissue their number one priority. Since muscle weighs more than fat, what you actually weigh is far less important than how it is *distributed* throughout the body. The majority of top-level athletes, including most volleyball players, would be considered overweight by American medical body weight charts. These charts and standards mean nothing to the competitive athlete and should be ignored. Remember, body composition is the *name of the game* in the sports world. Your body composition can be improved in a number of ways, many of which are listed in the following examples:

- Eat five or six smaller meals per day as opposed to the traditional three larger ones.

- Avoid eating heavy late at night before retiring. This means no midnight snacks or late night pizza binges.

- Eat high-fiber, reasonably low-fat meals as often as possible.

- Starchy carbohydrates such as pastas, white breads, and potatoes should be reasonably limited. (Remember, however, that hard-training athletes need energy to perform and workout, so it is recommended not to reduce starchy carbs drastically.)

- Get the majority of your protein from low-fat sources such as fish, lean meats, poultry, and egg whites.

- Avoid fried foods.

- Drink ample amounts of water throughout the day to flush your system.

- In addition to keeping your food intake light, engage in some form of aerobic exercise on a regular basis.

- Stay current with your strength training program. Building lean muscle onto your frame will help the body burn fat more efficiently.

- Stay clear of fad diets and diet pills.

- Lose fat/weight gradually—no more than three to five pounds per week.

Low Carbohydrate Diets

Low carbohydrate diets have become the rage of the weight-loss community in recent years. Some of the *benefits* of this type of diet according to its proponents include rapid weight loss, increased energy, and lowered cholesterol levels. Many nutritional experts, however, including those associated with the American Heart Association (AHA), are not yet *sold* on the low-carb approach and feel more research needs to be undertaken before it can be recommended.

Volleyball players, even if weight loss is their objective, should be very careful with low carbohydrate diets. These diets are usually geared to the extremely overweight, sedentary, or reasonable active lay person, not the hard-training, competitive athlete. Volleyball players need tremendous amounts of energy to perform and train at their best, so it stands to reason that depleting your body of its quintessential energy source (i.e., complex carbohydrates) should be undertaken with caution. If you do decide to experiment with any variation of a low carbohydrate diet, do so for only a short period of time (no longer than two weeks) and make sure to augment your eating with all the essential micronutrients that are found in fruits and vegetables via vitamin and mineral supplements.

Sample Meal Plans

Pre-Match Meal

Twenty years ago a pre-match meal consisted of a 12-ounce well-done steak, a baked potato piled high with sour cream, and if you were lucky, some type of vegetable. Eating a high-protein, high-fat pregame meal was the tradition in those days. What the sports community has learned over the years (thankfully) is that fatty foods are difficult to digest, thus consuming them can cause energy depletion, cramping, and discomfort. Not exactly what athletes are looking for prior to intense competition.

A pregame meal *should* include ample portions of complex carbohydrates, very little protein and fat, and large amounts of hydrating water. As mentioned earlier in this section, complex carbohydrates are easily digested and, when broken down, produce glucose, which supplies the body's energy needs. Before intense physical exertion, such as a volleyball match, having large amounts of energy at your disposal is obviously *crucial*. Pre-match meals should be planned three-and-a-half to four hours before competition.

Tables 3-1 through 3-4 detail sample meal plans for volleyball players. Keep in mind that the following meal plans are meant to be a basic guide only. What diet plan you follow will depend on numerous factors, including your food tastes, individual metabolism, activity level, and health variables.

- Three-quarter cup bowl of oatmeal with sliced banana and three ounces of 1% milk
- Four medium-sized whole wheat pancakes with maple syrup
- 12-ounce glass of orange juice
- 12-ounce glass of water

Table 3-1. Sample pre-match meal (afternoon match)

- Large bowl of whole wheat pasta (approximately five ounces)
- Large mixed salad
- Half a banana with peanut butter
- 12-ounce glass of grape juice
- 12-ounce glass of water

Table 3-2. Sample pre-match meal (night match)

Breakfast:	Three-egg (two yolks only) western omelet
	Two slices of dry whole-wheat or whole-grain toast
	One-half cup bowl of oatmeal with raisins and three ounces of 1% milk
	12-ounce glass of grapefruit juice
	12-ounce glass of water
Lunch:	Large turkey sandwich on rye bread with lettuce, tomato, and mustard
	Medium-sized bowl of vegetable soup
	Two 12-ounce glasses of water
Mid-Afternoon Snack:	Five whole-wheat crackers with peanut butter
	12-ounce glass of apple juice
Dinner:	Large piece of grilled fish (tuna, salmon, halibut, or swordfish)
	Baked potato with low-fat sour cream
	Large mixed salad with Italian dressing
	Slice of pound cake
	Two 12-ounce glasses of water
P.M. Snack:	Small slice of seven-grain bread with melted cheese
	Six-ounce glass of water

Table 3-3. Sample daily meal plan for volleyball players

Breakfast:	Six eggs scrambled (two yolks only)
	Two slices of whole-wheat or whole-grain toast with butter
	One-half cup bowl of oatmeal with two tablespoons of wheat germ and three ounces of whole milk
	12-ounce glass of orange juice
	12-ounce glass of water
Mid-Morning Snack:	Half-dozen saltine crackers spread with peanut butter
	Two 12-ounce glasses of water
Lunch:	Two medium-sized broiled skinless chicken breats
	One cup serving of brown rice
	Medium serving of grilled vegetables
	Two 12-ounce glasses of water
Mid-Afternoon Snack:	Serving of mixed nuts with dried fruit
	12-ounce glass of 2% milk
	12-ounce glass of water
Dinner:	12-ounce lean cut of beef
	Baked potato with sour cream
	Large mixed salad topped with hard cheese slices and dressing of choice
	Small container of low-fat yogurt
	Two 12-ounce glasses of water
P.M. Snack:	One slice of pound cake
	12-ounce glass of 1% milk with Ovaltine

Table 3-4. Sample daily weight-gain meal plan for volleyball players

PART II
VOLLEYBALL CONDITIONING

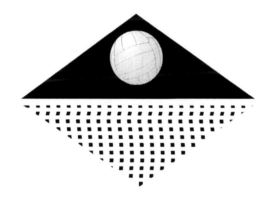

CHAPTER 4

Volleyball Conditioning Basics

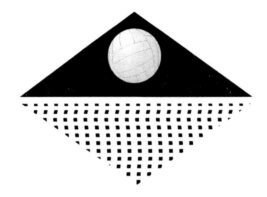

Before the specifics of how volleyball players should condition themselves for peak performance is reviewed, it is important that you have at least a fundamental understanding of the body's energy systems. This somewhat complex science of *energy systems* is explained in the following section.

Energy Systems

The energy released from the food you consume is utilized to manufacture a chemical compound called *adenosine triphosphate* or *ATP*. Muscle action is powered by the energy yielded from the hydrolysis of this compound. ATP can be produced by three pathways: two are considered *anaerobic* (without oxygen), the other *aerobic* (with oxygen).

The first pathway is called *ATP-PC* (phosphocreatine). PC, similar to ATP, is stored in the muscle and has an extremely high energy yield. The PC system itself is anaerobic, and the total amount of ATP that can be produced through this mechanism is finite. The ATP-PC pathway becomes involved when muscles are giving maximal effort, such as jumping as high as possible when attempting a block, performing a maximum weight lift, or sprinting 20 yards. The energy reserves from this system only last approximately 10 to 15 seconds.

The second pathway capable of producing ATP is termed *anaerobic glycolysis*—frequently referred to as the *lactic acid system*. This system, as the name suggests, is anaerobic and does not involve oxygen. During glycolysis, carbohydrates (glycogen or glucose) are broken down to form ATP.

Anaerobic glycolysis takes over where the ATP-PC system leaves off, allowing you to extend high-intensity exercise. However, be wary of limits as the buildup of lactic acid (lactate) triggers the commencement of fatigue (and the slowing of anaerobic glycolysis) usually, depending on the individual, within two-and-a-half minutes or so after the start of vigorous work. In essence, the process forces you to *discontinue* exercising, or at least lower the intensity considerably to facilitate the removal of lactic acid from the body. Examples that would bring this system into play include sprinting 400 meters or jumping rope *all-out* for two minutes.

The final pathway in the energy production chain is the *aerobic system*. This system supplies the body with long-term energy and involves the use of oxygen. After two-and-a-half to three minutes of exercise, the body's ATP requirements are met mostly by the aerobic system. Unlike glycolysis, which can only use carbohydrates to free energy, the aerobic metabolism is able to break down both fats and proteins along with carbohydrates to produce ATP. Some popular forms of aerobic exercise include long-distance jogging, swimming, and biking.

It is important to note that the transition between energy pathways is not an instantaneous change, but instead a *gradual shift* from one system to another. For example, when performing sand jumps with a weighted vest for 30 seconds, energy comes from a combination of the ATP-PC and the lactic acid system. In another example, the energy for sprinting 800 meters would come from both anaerobic pathways and the aerobic system. Table 4-1 gives an example of the *energy pathway continuum*.

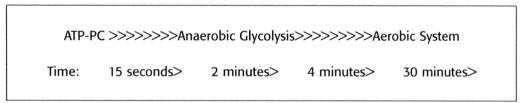

Table 4-1. Energy pathway continuum

Physical Fitness Volleyball-Style

Volleyball is a game of *reactive* movements—short, quick bursts of speed, and all-out, explosive jumps performed over and over and then over again. Therefore, the demands of the game from a physiological standpoint are mostly *anaerobic*. More specifically the ATP-PC system takes precedence, since the average point lasts somewhere between four and nine seconds, with the longest rallies lasting from 14 to 18 seconds. The correlating rest intervals between bouts of intense activity during a volleyball match average approximately 20 to 40 seconds.

These time parameters suggest that to condition the body for volleyball, conditioning drills should last no longer than 20 seconds and that an approximately *1:3 work/rest ratio* be employed. To some extent this is true, especially as you move closer to regular season competition. However, volleyball players, and all explosive-sport athletes for that matter, are best served working gradually through the conditioning continuum. This includes achieving an aerobic base early in the off-season, followed by longer-duration (45 seconds to 1.25 minutes) interval anaerobic workouts that focus on conditioning the lactic acid system, and finally culminating with volleyball specific ATP-PC system training (short bouts of exercise lasting 10 to 15 seconds) as the competitive campaign draws near. Many well-meaning volleyball coaches and conditioning specialists make the mistake of only prescribing short duration, ATP-PC system training to their athletes, neglecting completely the aerobic and lactic acid systems. This limited approach will not condition the volleyball player optimally, and may result in a training-related injury. Table 4-2 details how a volleyball player's conditioning should be structured on an annual basis.

Time of Year	System Trained
Early off-season	Aerobic
Early/mid off-season	Aerobic/Lactic Acid
Mid off-season	Lactic Acid
Late off-season	Lactic Acid/ATP-PC
Preseason	ATP-PC
In-season	ATP-PC

Table 4-2. Annual volleyball conditioning progression

Aerobic Training

Aerobic training is usually defined as any reasonably *low-intensity* (70 percent to 85 percent of your maximal heart rate) activity that is sustained for an *extended period of time*. Although some fitness professionals feel that aerobic benefits can be achieved in as little as 12 continuous minutes, for volleyball purposes it is best to work within 20-minute to 45-minute time parameters.

In addition to workout duration, the intensity at which you exercise must be taken into account. The simplest way to measure the intensity of an aerobic activity is by using percentages of your *maximum heart rate* (max HR). Your estimated max HR can be easily figured by subtracting your age from 220. An 18-year-old volleyball player, for example, would have a max HR of 202 (220-18 = 202). After determining your max HR, you can then find your suggested *aerobic training range*. Most experts agree that to acquire optimal aerobic benefits, you should train somewhere between 75 and 85 percent of your max HR. Using the previous example, 18-year-old athletes would need to elevate their heart rates between 151 and 172 *beats per minute* (bpm) to incur satisfactory aerobic conditioning benefits. Of course, much depends upon the duration of the activity, the particular mode of aerobic exercise, and the genetic capacity of the individual.

Your heart rate can be conveniently calculated by using a *heart rate monitor*. These devices can be purchased at a fairly nominal cost at most sporting goods and fitness stores, or through a fitness equipment catalog. If a heart monitor is not available, you can determine your heart rate by simply checking your pulse rate by pinpointing your radial artery in your wrist and counting the bpm.

Volleyball Players Should Not Neglect Aerobic Training

Aerobic training has gone through a number of public relations transformations over the years. When it first came on the scene it was regarded as perhaps the perfect fitness tool, favored by athletes such as basketball and soccer players for its conditioning benefits as well as by the general public for its health-promoting qualities.

Over the past 10 years or so the attitude toward aerobic training has changed considerably, especially among those in the sports-training community. While the proven health benefits of enhanced cardiorespiratory function, elevated HDL cholesterol (the *good* cholesterol), and lower blood pressure are not disputed, engaging in excessive amounts of aerobic training has shown to be somewhat *problematic* for explosive sport athletes like volleyball players. Some of the negative byproducts include inhibiting jumping ability, explosive speed, and quickness—not exactly what volleyball players are looking for from their training—and the loss of hard-earned muscle mass. Additionally, the repetitive pounding of high-impact aerobic activities such as long-distance jogging, especially when executed on hard surfaces such as pavement, can lead to joint problems. As if all that wasn't enough, too much aerobic training has a tendency to *wear the body down*, leaving it susceptible to overtraining-related injuries and general fatigue.

But before you rush downstairs to the basement and begin dismantling your father's old stationary bike, keep in mind that while aerobic training is not the fitness panacea it was once thought to be, neither is it a worthless conditioning method that will ruin your volleyball game. The truth is that aerobic exercise, if employed properly and in reasonable moderation, can be a *useful component* of a volleyball player's year-round conditioning program. The following are just a few reasons why:

- *Provides a conditioning base*: To prepare your body for intense anaerobic, volleyball specific workouts, you must first develop a solid base of conditioning. Aerobic training provides this base. In essence, aerobic training sets the stage for subsequent anaerobic workouts. Those who attempt to jump right into anaerobic/volleyball training sessions without any preconditioning are setting themselves up for failure, not to mention injury.

- *Improves recovery time*: Anyone who has played competitive volleyball knows that huffing, puffing, and gasping for air is not the ideal way to begin a point. Achieving a high-degree of aerobic fitness will enhance your ability to recover during stoppages in play (between points, games, and during time-outs), ensuring peak levels of performance throughout a match. This enhanced ability to recover is not limited to volleyball competitions; strength, plyometric, and agility workouts will be similarly improved. Aerobic training has also been shown to improve long-term recuperation (24 to 72 hours) by assisting in the removal of lactic acid from the system after intense physical activity.

- *Weight control*: Aerobic exercise speeds up the metabolism, turning the body into a virtual fat-burning furnace. If you tend to put on unwanted weight, regular aerobic training combined with a low-calorie diet will counteract this condition. While it's not recommended for volleyball players to perform aerobic training during the competitive season, if excess weight is inhibiting performance exceptions can and should be made.

- *Maintains condition during down time*: There will be times over the course of a volleyball player's training year that engaging in fast-paced, high-intensity activities like plyometrics or agility training will not be an option—for instance, when recovering from a lower leg injury such as a sprained ankle or stress fracture. In this case and others, non-impact aerobic training (stationary biking, swimming, rowing, etc.) can be used to maintain adequate levels of physical conditioning until you're ready to resume more demanding workouts.

- *Perform better late*: Being in aerobic shape will allow you to perform at peak levels at the end of a match and toward the later stages of the competitive campaign. Players who are strong in late-game and season situations are usually the ones who've conditioned their aerobic systems diligently.

Eight-Week Aerobic Conditioning Program

Table 4-3 illustrates a *sample aerobic conditioning program* for volleyball players. The program should commence approximately four weeks or so after your competitive season ends. The sessions are designed to gradually build up aerobic capacity by slowly increasing workout duration and workouts per week. During the last two weeks of the eight-week program, transition workouts will be incorporated where you will combine aerobic training with low-intensity anaerobic exercise.

Week 1:	Monday	20 minutes	Friday	22 minutes
Week 2:	Sunday Tuesday	24 minutes 25 minutes	Friday	26 minutes
Week 3:	Sunday Tuesday	28 minutes 30 minutes	Friday	30 minutes
Week 4:	Sunday Tuesday	32 minutes 34 minutes	Saturday	34 minutes
Week 5:	Monday Wednesday	35 minutes 36 minutes	Thursday Saturday	36 minutes 38 minutes
Week 6:	Monday Tuesday	40 minutes 40 minutes	Thursday Saturday	40 minutes 40 minutes
Week 7:	Tuesday Friday	35 minutes/low-intensity anaerobic workout 30 minutes/low-intensity anaerobic workout		
Week 8:	Tuesday Friday	30 minutes/low-intensity anaerobic workout 30 minutes/low-intensity anaerobic workout		

Table 4-3. Sample eight-week aerobic conditioning program

CHAPTER 5

Anaerobic Training

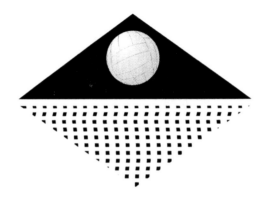

Physical activity is considered *anaerobic* when you are exercising at about 85 to 100 percent of your maximum heart rate. The following instances are examples where volleyball players work anaerobically during competition: exploding upward for a spike, sliding laterally to dig a hard hit jump serve, and sprinting full speed beyond the baseline in pursuit of a miss-hit ball.

The key to successful anaerobic workouts is *intensity*. You must work as hard as possible for the prescribed time and/or distance. As discussed previously, the high-effort nature of anaerobic training will allow you to exercise only in short bouts, two-and-a-half minutes being the maximum, before fatigue gets the best of you. Although some suggest that you should monitor your heart rate during anaerobic training sessions, it is not always necessary, as the pain in your lungs and legs should let you know in short order if you're in your *anaerobic training zone*.

Anaerobic Training for Volleyball

As mentioned earlier, many in the volleyball and conditioning communities feel that since the bouts of activity in a volleyball match usually last somewhere between 4 and

18 seconds, only the ATP-PC should be regularly conditioned. Not everyone, including this author, agrees with this point of view. Volleyball players should fully condition their *entire anaerobic system,* both lactic acid and ATP-PC, in an organized and progressive manner. Not doing so will hinder performance, especially when it counts most at the conclusion of matches and at the end of a long grueling volleyball season.

The recommended anaerobic training program for volleyball lasts for 16 weeks, beginning at the conclusion of your aerobic program and continuing until right before regular season practice begins. Workouts should be accomplished two non-consecutive days per week, and there will be one rest week in the middle of the program. In the event that you participate in numerous off-season volleyball leagues or partake regularly in additional anaerobic activities such as full-court basketball, you may want to cut back your organized anaerobic workouts to once per week periodically. On the other hand, if you engage in little additional anaerobic activities during the off-season, it is recommended that you add a third anaerobic session to your week.

Work:Rest Ratios

When designing anaerobic conditioning programs for volleyball, it is critical that specific *work:rest ratios* be incorporated. The work:rest ratio denotes the work or exercise period of an activity relative to the rest interval. For example, if you sprint for 50 seconds and then rest for 100 seconds before sprinting again, your work:rest ratio would be 1:2.

Typically, the longer the bout of anaerobic activity, the smaller the work:rest ratio. For instance, going all-out on a stationary bike during a *spinning* class for two minutes requires approximately a work:rest ratio of 1:1. At the other end of the spectrum, sprinting up a steep grade hill for 15 seconds would call for a work:rest ratio of about 1:3. Table 5-1 summarizes the various durations for anaerobic training and the appropriate work:rest ratios involved.

Work/Time in Seconds	Work:Rest Ratios
0 to 45	1:3
45 to 120	1:2 to 1:1
120 to 150	1:1

Table 5-1. Anaerobic exercise times and approximate work:rest ratios

Sample 16-Week Anaerobic Training Program

Table 5-2 details a sample 16-week anaerobic conditioning program for volleyball based on two workouts per week performed on non-consecutive days.

Week	Sets per Workout	Exercise Duration	Rest
#1	3	75 seconds	3 minutes
#2	4	75 seconds	2.5 minutes
#3	5	60 seconds	2.25 minutes
#4	5	60 seconds	2.25 minutes
#5	6	45 seconds	2 minutes
#6	7	45 seconds	1.75 minutes
#7	8	35 seconds	1.5 minutes
#8	8	30 seconds	1.25 minutes
#9	8	30 seconds	1.25 minutes
#10	Rest Week		
#11	10	25 seconds	70 seconds
#12	10	25 seconds	70 seconds
#13	12	20 seconds	60 seconds
#14	14	15 seconds	45 seconds
#15	15	15 seconds	45 seconds
#16	20	10 seconds	30 seconds

Table 5-2. Sample 16-week anaerobic training program

Modes of Volleyball Conditioning

Due to the popularity of physical conditioning among both the athletic community and the general public over the past two-and-a-half decades, an almost endless number of options are at your disposal when it comes to training your aerobic and anaerobic systems. Walk into any commercial fitness center or athletic training facility these days, and you'll immediately see a dizzying array of cardiovascular exercise equipment. The *choice* of how you condition your aerobic and anaerobic systems is ultimately up to you. The following are some detailed favorites. The only prerequisite is that you follow the time-and-effort/heart rate recommendations discussed earlier in the book.

Running

Running is covered first in this section because, simply stated, *it works*. Running is, in the opinion of most sports-training specialists, the *best* form of conditioning for explosive sport athletes. After all, explosive sports, including volleyball, are performed on your feet, so it stands to reason that a training method where you move from place to place in an erect position would be most desirable.

In addition to its tremendous physical-conditioning qualities, running also yields *positive* psychological effects. Traversing along a scenic path or beach does wonders for your state of mind. And it makes no difference whether you're training your anaerobic system with explosive 20-yard sprints or your aerobic metabolism with a slow-paced four-mile jog. The results to your mind-set are the same. If possible, try to get the majority of your early and mid off-season running sessions accomplished outdoors. This is rewarding for both mind and body, especially after being cooped up in a gymnasium all season long.

As with all training modalities, running is not without its drawbacks. Most notably, it is hard on the knees, feet, and lower back, as the constant pounding from foot fall after foot fall takes its toll on the body. This can be alleviated somewhat by keeping your running workouts to *soft surfaces* such as rubberized running tracks, turf fields, and low-cut grass. Pavement and other hard, non-giving terrain should be avoided for running workouts.

If you have a history of impact-related injuries or weigh more than 225 pounds, treadmill running may be for you. Treadmills have soft running surfaces and allow you to alternate speeds and grades easily, making workouts generally less stressful on the body. Some reasonably new workout machines are also less stressful on the body, like the elliptical trainer that simulates the running motion without the inherent impact. However, these pieces of equipment, while certainly non-impact, fail to produce the fitness gains of conventional running. The following are some helpful tips to keep you running injury free:

- *Use proper footwear*: It is imperative that you have running shoes that fit, are comfortable, and, most important, are not worn out. It's amazing how many competitive athletes allow their running footwear to deteriorate to the point where using them for workouts becomes downright dangerous. A variety of injuries including ankle sprains, knee twists, and stress fractures could be avoided by simply keeping your running shoes up to date. It is recommended that you maintain two or even three pairs off running footwear at all times, rotating them every third workout or so. When they show any signs of wearing down, replace them immediately. Although this approach can get somewhat expensive, it will be well worth the price in terms of preventing injury.

- *Build up gradually*: All running programs should be taken on gradually. Advancing too fast before you're ready increases the risk of injury substantially. Most injuries—whether sustained on the volleyball court, weight room, or running track—occur when the body is fatigued. Following the conditioning programs in this book will ensure that you progress optimally and safely with your running program.

- *Keep to soft surfaces*: This topic was previously covered, but it's important to re-emphasize the point of executing your running workouts on soft surfaces. Interestingly, the popularity of running as a conditioning tool and health promoter is partially to blame for runners hitting the hard streets for their workouts. Proponents have long exposed the numerous benefits running provides including its relative convenience. No long drives to the gym, expensive equipment, or complicated movements to learn—just straight out the front door and off you go. The problem is that straight out the door for most people means sidewalks and paved streets, not soft running tracks and manicured grass. You should always make running a focal | point of your conditioning routine, but try to stay on soft surfaces.

- *Awareness of minor discomforts*: Most regular runners develop an instinctive feel for when slight discomforts have the potential to become problematic injuries. For instance, when you feel a minor sensation in the front of your lower leg, it may be a precursor to a debilitating case of shin splints. If you plan on making running a major part of your training regime, you too must develop this innate feel for oncoming injuries and act accordingly. Acting accordingly may entail discontinuing a particular run when discomfort occurs or switching to a less taxing training modality such as stationary biking for a few workouts until the problem dissipates.

- *Stretch before and after*: Stretching before and after all training sessions or competitions is a prerequisite for volleyball players. Nowhere is it more important than before and after running workouts. Stretching prior to running loosens and warms the muscles that help to prevent muscle pulls and strains. Post-workout flexibility work enhances recovery and gets you ready for your next injury free run.

Stationary Biking

Riding a stationary bike has long been a popular form of exercise for athletes and non-athletes alike. It is a low-impact activity, requires little in the way of expertise, and offers a method of exercising where the intensity can be easily regulated. With the exception of swimming and pool work, it is the most *accepted* activity prescribed for injured athletes and for athletes returning after long layoffs.

The key to successful stationary bike workouts lies in *sustaining your target heart rate*. Where swimming and running, for example, tend to elevate the heart rate to appropriate levels without much conscious effort, biking, especially stationary biking, requires full concentration to maintain a target heart rate (70 to 85 percent of max HR for aerobic benefits; 85 to 100 percent of max HR for anaerobic training purposes). Because of this, it is recommended that you incorporate a heart rate monitor during all stationary bike sessions. Two activities that are discouraged when training on a stationary bike are reading and watching television. Although convenient and time-passing endeavors, both take your attention away from the task at hand, which is of course getting the most productive conditioning workout possible.

Numerous types of stationary bikes are available to you. They run the gamut from fancy, computerized models that gauge just about everything (i.e., heart rate, calories burned, revolutions per minute, miles traveled, etc.) to the simple, hand-operated original that is probably gathering dust in your attic. Computerized stationary bikes are preferred by most, but all styles can be utilized for effective workouts. Just make sure the bike is comfortable, has an easily adjustable seat, durable pedals, and that tension can be calibrated smoothly. Keep in mind that if you decide to buy a computerized bike for your home, parts and maintenance can be very expensive and are not always available in a timely manner.

Stationary bike workout classes known as *spinning* have become popular at gyms and health clubs through the years. These organized training sessions consist of an instructor leading a group through an interval workout where intensities are constantly changed. These workouts can be extremely beneficial for both the aerobic and lactic acid systems, especially if the instructor is experienced and is aware of your training objectives.

Swimming

Regardless of your proficiency as a swimmer, hitting the pool for a workout has many benefits. Swimming furnishes a *fantastic full-body workout*, as virtually every muscle in the arms, legs, and torso are involved to some degree. It provides terrific aerobic and anaerobic training benefits, and swimming contributes to loosening and toning the muscles of the upper body. (One look at the physiques of world class swimmers and you'll see all have broad backs, slim waists, and muscular shoulders.) And the best news of all for volleyball players concerning water training is that regardless if you're swimming, running in the pool (a popular form of exercise in the sports community currently), or just treading water, it is extremely easy on the joints, offering perhaps the ultimate low-impact workout. Because of this, pool workouts are universally recognized as the most efficient way for injured athletes to maintain their conditioning during downtime. Most major college sports programs have specially designed water-training protocols for their injured athletes to follow.

If your swimming skills leave something to be desired, don't be discouraged; you have a plethora of accessories to choose from such as kickboards and flotation vests that will keep your head above water. So by all means experiment periodically with water training and give your body a well-deserved break from the pounding of the hard courts.

Nordic Tracking

The Nordic Track is an exercise machine that simulates *cross-country skiing*. What in the world does cross-country skiing have to do with volleyball you ask? Very little of course, however, volleyball players, along with all movement-intensive sport athletes, can benefit greatly by incorporating this exercise into their training programs. In fact, it is a widely held belief among exercise physiologists that elite Nordic skiers are among the finest conditioned athletes in all of sports. Many of these athletes spend a good deal of workout time on the Nordic Track.

The machine itself provides a terrific low-impact workout that places negligible strain on the knees and lower back. It exercises the upper and lower body in unison, thus adding to the intensity of the workout, and is great for anaerobic interval training. The only drawback of the Nordic Track is that it takes some getting used to in terms of execution, especially if like most volleyball players, you've not spent much time on skies. After a few sessions, however, most athletes get comfortable enough on the machine to enjoy productive workouts. The majority of health clubs and fitness centers feature some variation of a cross-country ski machine. The Nordic Track is the best piece of conditioning equipment for your home—that is, if you can get it through the front door.

Rowing

World-class rowers, similar to the previously mentioned Nordic skiers, are known for their *high levels of physical conditioning*. They consistently score high on all varieties of cardiovascular fitness tests, and their training regimes are viewed by many as the most demanding in all competitive athletics.

For most of you, rowing workouts will be accomplished indoors on a rowing machine. While rowing on a lake or river is extremely pleasant and exhilarating, most volleyball players don't have the time or inclination to perfect the requisite skills to row outdoors.

Indoors or outdoors, rowing is an extraordinary exercise. It works all the major muscles groups in the body, with an emphasis on the back and biceps. When performed at the appropriate intensity, rowing allows for excellent aerobic and anaerobic workouts. Additionally, rowing is low impact and relatively easy to learn.

The two standard types of rowing machines are the *hydraulic cylinder rowers* and *flywheel rowers*. Both machines are adequate, but many fitness professionals prefer the flywheel model because it simulates water rowing to a greater degree and places slightly less stress on the lower back.

Before engaging in intense workouts on the rowing machine, it is imperative that you thoroughly warm up and stretch your entire back region. Rowing puts a fair amount of strain on this area, so it is best to be careful. If you have a history of lower back problems, rowing should not be part of your conditioning program.

PART III
STRENGTH TRAINING FOR VOLLEYBALL

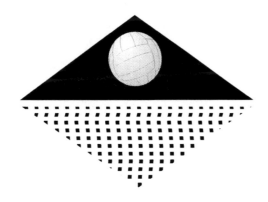

CHAPTER 6

Volleyball Strength Training Basics and Principles

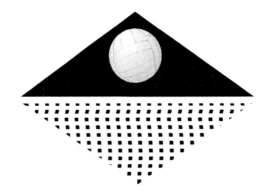

Strength training used to be taboo throughout the majority of the sports world not too long ago. The weight room was a place for bodybuilders and competitive weight lifters. Other individual and team-sport athletes were, for the most part, discouraged from *pumping iron*. Strength training was said to cause a variety of performance inhibiting byproducts including decreased speed, quickness, and agility, unwanted bulk, reduced flexibility, and diminished coordination. As if all of these weren't enough, the experts of the day postulated that strength training regularly would eventually result in serious injury.

Despite the widely held concerns, some power-sport athletes such as football players, wrestlers, and shot putters slowly began to dip their toes in the water and experiment with weights. Surprisingly to some, these individuals not only failed to experience any of the negative consequences previously mentioned, but showed vast improvements in strength, power, and general athletic performance. With the genie finally out of the bottle, finesse-sport athletes (basketball players, baseball players, tennis players, and even golfers) got into the act. They too showed performance increases with no ill effects. Strength training was here to stay in the sports world.

Why Strength Train for Volleyball?

Strength training today is a *staple* for most all-competitive athletes including volleyball players. It has many byproducts that can enhance your performance on the volleyball court. For example, you will become more explosive in your movements, whether rising for a powerful spike or lunging to the floor for a hard hit ball. Your speed and quickness will improve, especially those all-important first few steps. You will find yourself jumping higher and getting off the floor quicker. Your stamina and endurance will be much enhanced and will enable you to perform at peak-performance levels during the last few points of an intense match and at the end of a long, grueling volleyball season.

Training with weights is also your *best defense against injury*, as stronger muscles allow you to withstand the rigors of two-a-day practice sessions and exhausting competitive matches. Additional muscle mass built in the weight room will also improve your ability to absorb contact, so those headlong dives to the floor will be less taxing on your body. And as a direct result of lifting weights and becoming stronger, your confidence in yourself and your volleyball game will increase dramatically.

Strength training promotes *team camaraderie* as well. The weight room or team-training facility is a sanctuary where athletes can workout in a congenial atmosphere, away from the critical eye of coaches. Teammates can encourage each other to give their best efforts. In the process, they'll become generally closer as a ball club, which as anyone who is involved in sports knows is a key ingredient to a successful team. Furthermore, if a player desires to add lean body weight, combining strength training with a healthy high-calorie diet is the ticket. Conversely, if losing weight is your aim, training with weights and building additional muscle increases the metabolic rate, an important component in burning fat more efficiently. While you will achieve plenty of other benefits by strength training, the aforementioned should be more than enough to convince you to hit the weights.

One point worth emphasizing before moving ahead to the basics of volleyball strength training is that while strength training is an extremely important component of a volleyball player's year-round improvement program, it should be used as a *supplement* to your on-court work. The goal is *not* to become an Olympic weightlifter or bodybuilding champion. All the weight training in the world will mean nothing to your performance in-between the lines unless you diligently work on your game. Remember, skill development comes first; strength and conditioning an important second. Working out with weights and getting stronger is a great way to gain an edge on the competition. Just keep it in perspective.

Strength Training Basics

Before beginning your strength training program, you must first become familiar with the *basic aspects* of working out with weights. The following information will help you get started on the right track.

Weight Training Equipment

You should use two types of weight training equipment: *free weights* (accompanied by a variety of exercise benches and power racks), and a selection of *weight machines*. Most gyms and team-training facilities have a full compliment of each type. Free weight equipment consists of barbells and dumbbells. A good exercise bench should be sturdy and easily adjustable, allowing for different incline positions. Power racks are used for squatting and other heavy-standing movements (i.e., hang cleans, push presses, barbell shrugs, etc.). A substantial number of strength training machines are available for your use. The most useful are the lat machine, leg press, cable row, leg extension, leg curl, and pullover machine.

Attire

- *Clothing*: Loose, comfortable fitting clothing is best for strength training. What you wear on the volleyball court is fine. The most important thing is that your clothing does not in any way hinder your movement and exercise performance. In a cold gym, it is suggested that you wear some type of sweat suit, at least until your body warms up.

- *Footwear*: Some footwear is specifically designed for weightlifting. However, most volleyball, basketball, or cross-training sneakers are suitable. Running or jogging shoes lack lateral support and should not be worn in the weight room.

- *Gloves*: Many bodybuilders and other regular weight trainers prefer to wear weightlifting gloves during their strength workouts. Some feel gloves provide a better grip, and they do help to prevent calluses from developing on your hands, but they are not necessary to the workout itself and are probably a waste of money.

- *Weightlifting belt*: A weightlifting belt is typically four to eight inches wide and made of leather or nylon. Belts are designed to support the lower back during heavy lifts. Although some trainers and conditioning specialists feel weight belts are not necessary, and that their benefit is mostly psychological, it is still recommended you wear one during heavy-standing lifts.

- *Straps*: Straps are used mostly by bodybuilders to prevent grip fatigue during exercises, such as chin-ups and upright rows. Volleyball players have no need for straps in their strength training workouts.

- *Waist harness*: A waist harness allows you to add weight to your frame when performing exercises like dips, push-ups, and chin-ups.

Safety

- *Warm-up*: If you hope to reduce your chances of suffering a strength training injury, you must be sufficiently warmed up before each and every weight workout. Warming up was discussed in detail in Chapter 2.

- *Use spotters*: It is essential that a spotter be used when you are performing heavy sets of bench presses, incline presses, shoulder presses, and squats. This rule has no exceptions. Neglecting this advice can result in serious injury. In addition to ensuring your safety, an attentive, knowledgeable spotter can correct errors in lifting form and help you to get the most out of a set by giving just enough assistance to enable you to complete that final repetition.

- *Heavy singles*: Many strength training-induced injuries would be prevented if one-repetition lifts were avoided. Besides trying to impress your friends in the gym, absolutely no reason exists to perform heavy singles. Three or four repetition sets are far superior to maximum-weight single lifts for building strength, power, and muscle.

- *Collars*: You should get in the habit of using collars for all barbell lifts. They will ensure that weight plates do not slide and cause you to lose control of the bar.

- *Check equipment*: All equipment should be checked for safety before use. For example, make sure that benches are sturdy, plates are tight to the bar, machine cables are not worn out, and all collars are secure.

- *Be aware*: It is important that you are aware of what's going on around you in the weight room, especially if it's crowded. Although you may be following all the proper weight training protocol, other exercisers may not be, so keep your eyes open to prevent a mishap.

Weight Room Etiquette

If you're going to be a regular in the weight room, which you will be if your coaches have anything to do about it, learning proper etiquette is a *must*. Following the simple rules of weight room conduct will go a long way toward making your (and others) strength training experience a productive and pleasant one.

- *Abstain from horseplay*: Fooling around during your strength sessions will not only hinder your progress, it can be downright dangerous to you and those around you. So do yourself and everybody else a favor, save the horseplay for after the workout.

- *Replace all weights after use*: If you've ever been in a gym or weight room where weight plates were scattered about, machine pins missing, and dumbbells covering the floor, you know how unpleasant this workout environment can be. It is imperative that you replace all weights, bars, and any other equipment to their proper place after each use. Pay particular attention to returning dumbbells and barbell plates to their weight appropriate racks. Most public fitness centers and gyms have signs posted reminding members to replace all weights after use. Take heed of this advice and replace all equipment after you're finished with it.

- *Let others work in*: If you're working out in a crowed public gym more often than not someone will want to alternate sets with you. Although this may be somewhat disruptive to the pace of your workout, proper weight room protocol calls for you to let others work in. Of course, if you're training with a partner, this won't be a problem.

- *Wipe down all equipment after use*: Nobody wants to workout on wet, sweaty equipment. After you conclude your sets be sure to towel down the equipment for the next person.

Strength Training Principles

- *Sets and repetitions*: Sets and repetitions are the units of measure used in strength training. For example, bench pressing a barbell eight consecutive times with only a brief pause in-between lifts constitutes one set of eight repetitions. The simple notation used to indicate such a performance is *1 x 8*. The first number listed always represents sets, and the second figure represents *repetitions*.

- *Multi-joint exercises*: Multi-joint exercises work more than one muscle group at a time. An example of a multi-joint exercise is the high pull, which exercises a variety of muscle groups including the deltoids, legs, forearms, biceps, and lower back. These types of movements should be the focal point of your strength program.

- *Single-joint exercises*: Sometimes referred to as *auxiliary exercises*, single-joint movements work one muscle group at a time. Two examples of single-joint exercises are dumbbell curls for the biceps and lateral raises for the deltoids. These exercises will supplement the multi-joint movements in your strength program.

- *Train your largest muscle groups first*: It is important that you train your largest muscles first in your strength workouts. Two basic reasons are behind this idea. First, the smaller muscle is already the weak link in the strength chain when executing any multi-joint lift. In the incline press, for example, training the triceps before incline pressing would further weaken the smaller muscle (triceps) thus limiting the workload for the area of the body you are attempting to exercise (upper chest). Second, the bigger the body part, the more energy it takes to train. Because your energy levels are obviously higher at the beginning of a workout, it is best to exercise larger muscles (hips, legs, upper back) first in your weight training sessions.

- *Pyramid sets*: For the most effective results from your strength training efforts, it is recommended that you incorporate pyramid sets within your workout. As the term suggests, pyramiding entails progressing from lighter weight sets to your heaviest set, then lowering the resistance on your last set or two. The notation would look something like this: 1 x 15, 1 x 10, 1 x 6, 1 x 8, 1 x 10. Training in this manner will help ensure maximum muscle fatigue and strength gains.

- *Strength progression*: The major premise of sound strength training is obviously progression. To encourage this, it is best to perform the majority of your sets (not including warm-up sets) near the point of muscular failure. For instance, if your program calls for a 10-repetition set, you would choose a weight that allows you to complete 10 repetitions and no more. When more than 10 repetitions can be executed in good form, it is time to add weight. Usually a five-percent increase is sufficient for multi-joint exercises.

    Of course finding the appropriate resistance level for each exercise in your program will require a period of trial and error, especially if you're new to strength training or coming off a long layoff. Keep in mind that strength progression usually comes quickly for beginners. It is not unusual for a novice strength trainer to make substantial gains in strength and muscle in as little as three short months. Unfortunately, as times goes on, and your body becomes accustomed to pumping iron, increases in strength become more difficult. Progression is still possible, however, albeit at a slower pace, and should continue to be a priority.

- *Consistency*: If you hope to reach your strength potential, you must be consistent. This may seem obvious and not worth mentioning, but consistency is so vital to the strength-building process that without it failure is not only possible but assured. You must push yourself to get to the gym or training facility regularly and then proceed to work hard when you get there. Even missing a few scheduled workouts can set you back substantially. Lifting weights more so than any other conditioning discipline is cumulative. The weight you lift this week is directly correlated to the weight you lifted the previous week and so on down the line. When it comes to building strength and muscle, no shortcuts and no exceptions exist.

- *Concentration*: Concentration is an often-overlooked aspect of strength training. It is, however, of paramount importance. You must aspire to bring full concentration to every exercise, set, and repetition during your strength workout. This, of course, is easier said than done, given the fact that the mind can wander off in a million different directions. Unlike participating in a match or practice, where concentration comes about naturally due to outside stimuli, training with weights is personal undertaking that demands constant and mindful attention. So keep your concentration focused on the task at hand in the weight room, and watch as your workouts become ever more productive.

- *Breathing*: Typically, you will find it easier to inhale during the lowering phase of an exercise and to breathe out during the lifting or work phase of the movement. Many athletes and trainers have found that when training with weights their breathing tends to regulate naturally without much conscious thought. Obviously, you should never hold your breath when lifting weights.

- *Rest between sets*: How much you rest between sets mostly relates to how heavy you are lifting. During heavy training sessions, you should rest up to three minutes before attempting a subsequent set. If you're working with light or medium weights, anywhere from one to two minutes is usually sufficient. Mixing up your rest intervals over the course of a workout is a great way to add variety to your training and can lead to overall strength gains.

- *Lifting speed*: When it comes to the speed of individual repetitions, many contrasting views exist. Some experts feel lifting in a rapid fashion is more conducive to the needs of a volleyball player. Others believe that slower lifting allows a larger number of muscle fibers to come in to play, thus developing more strength. You might want to come down somewhere in the middle. Unless you are executing explosive-type lifts that require high levels of repetition speed or specialized techniques, such as forced repetitions or negative repetitions where slow repetitions are employed, it is recommended that you lift in a powerful, yet controlled manner without sacrificing proper exercise form.

- *Muscle balance*: While some muscle groups are more essential to volleyball performance than others, it is nevertheless of paramount importance that you achieve balanced muscular development. When antagonist muscle groups, such as quadriceps and hamstrings or chest and upper back, are out of balance strength wise, coordination and performance can suffer. You also become more vulnerable to injury.

- *Record keeping*: It is extremely important that you maintain accurate records concerning your strength training. At the very least, you should keep a training log that includes the date of workouts, exercises, exercise order, weights, sets, repetitions, rest between sets, and total workout duration.

- *Variety*: Never has the saying "variety is the spice of life" been more appropriate as to when it relates to strength training. Mixing up your workout routine is *essential* to continued progress. A number of reasons can be listed to support this factor.

    First, changing your routine periodically keeps your muscles off balance, forcing them to adjust to the new demands placed upon them, thus producing gains in strength. The body adapts fairly quickly, especially if you've been training consistently for a number of years, and must be constantly challenged with new stimuli to improve.

    Second, incorporating different exercises, set sequences, repetition schemes, and training intensities enables your workouts to be more interesting and creative. The tediousness of performing the same workout week after week and month after month can take its toll on even the most dedicated athlete.

    Finally, being flexible with your training will also help you avoid overuse injuries. Working muscles, tendons, ligaments, and joints from the same angle with the same exercises for an extended number of workouts can eventually lead to injury.

- *Limitations*: No matter how great your potential, at some point, you will hit your limit. It may seem odd to bring up limitations in a book dedicated to improvement, but realizing your strengths and weaknesses (and yes, even your limits) is an important factor in getting the most out of your strength program. Having unrealistic expectations can be as dangerous to your progress as setting lackluster goals. You must understand that genetics, like it or not, play a major role in muscle and strength development. The key is to appreciate the improvement you make without becoming frustrated because you don't look like Arnold Schwarzenegger after a year of strength training.

Training the Core

The power for all explosive athletic movements either emanates or is transferred through the *core of the body* (midsection, hips, and lower back). Because of this, it is the most important part of the physique when it comes to volleyball performance. A strong core also contributes to the prevention of injury. Not surprisingly, core training will be the focal point of a volleyball player's strength training program.

Core Training Secrets and Suggestions

- *Core strength comes first:* A solid base of core conditioning should be attained prior to engaging in intense, full-body strength training. One way to achieve this is to focus exclusively on core-strengthening movements for the first three weeks or so of your off-season strength program. It is recommended that all volleyball players have a minimum of six lower back and 10 to 12 abdominal training sessions under their belts before stepping into a squat rack or lifting a barbell off the floor.

- *Strengthen the core gradually*: Core strengthening should always be undertaken gradually. Progressing too fast, especially with lower back training, will put you at risk for injury. And unlike many other workout-related injuries, lower back ailments can become chronic and keep you out of action for extended periods of time. So take care to move ahead deliberately with your core training by first focusing on simpler, less taxing movements such as crunches, floor back raises, and lightweight good mornings, before moving on to more complicated and demanding exercises like weighted prone hyperextensions and hanging leg raises.

- *The midsection can be trained more frequently than the lower back and hips*: The lower back and hips can take considerable time to recover from intense training. A minimum of 72 hours and up to 96 hours between hip and lower back workouts may be necessary depending upon individual recovery requirements. On the other hand, abdominal muscles recover quite rapidly and can be exercised up to 5 days per week at reasonable levels of intensity. (Some elite, highly conditioned athletes actually train their midsections on a daily basis.) In light of these recovery variables, it is recommended that volleyball players train the low back and hips no more than twice per week, while exercising the midsection four days per week. Adhering to this core training schedule will ensure strength balance, along with preventing overtraining-related injury.

- *Combine direct lower back work with leg training*: Multi-joint leg exercises such as squats and straight-legged dead lifts work the entire lower back region significantly. In fact, regardless of how strong your quadriceps, hips, and hamstrings are, a weak lower back will ensure that you'll never reach your potential in these important lifts. Considering how the lower back, hips, and legs work in tandem both in the weight room and on the volleyball court, it is strongly recommended that you train these areas together in the same workout. Perform the more energy intensive movements (squats, lunges, step-ups, etc.) first in the session, followed by direct lower back exercises (good mornings, reverse back raises, prone hyperextensions, etc.) Approaching your lower back training in this manner will ensure that adequate recovery is afforded and overtraining avoided.

- *Feel the burn*: While some people don't subscribe to the, *no pain, no gain* theory of physical conditioning, you should make an exception with abdominal training. When you exercise your midsection, the goal is to feel the muscles work. This unpleasant sensation signals that the muscles of the midsection are contracting and being stimulated, and is unfortunately a necessary evil for productive abdominal workouts. Keep in mind also that athletes with disparate body types may respond differently to the same abdominal movements. It is your responsibility to find out which midsection exercises work best for you and which ones are a waste of your time and energy. This anti-one-size-fits-all approach to abdominal training will ensure that your midsection becomes strong, toned, and functional.

Core Exercises

Bench Crunch

Muscles worked: Upper abdominal region

Exercise type: Single-joint

Movement execution: Lying on your back with your hands clasped behind your head, place your feet and lower legs over a flat exercise bench. Proceed to sit up, raising your head toward your knees. Pause momentarily at the top, and lower your body under control back to the floor.

Training tips and variations: This exercise can be performed without the bench by placing your feet flat on the floor with your legs bent at the knees. You can also find a number of exercise machines that simulate the crunching motion. To engage more of the lower midsection, lift your pelvis off the floor during the up phase of the movement. For added resistance, hold a barbell plate or medicine ball behind your head.

 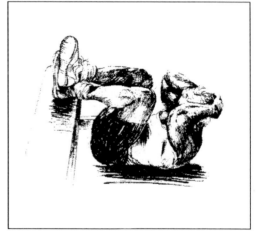

Leg-in-the-Air Sit-Ups

Muscles worked: Lower abdominal region

Exercise type: Single-joint

Movement execution: Lying on your back with your hands clasped behind your head, hold your legs in the air as high as possible. From there, crunch up, and bring your head to your knees. Hold for a count at the top and then lower yourself back to the starting position.

Training tips and variations: Although your concentration should be on working your lower abdominal area, you can, by bending your knees, exercise your upper midsection more directly. Similar to bench crunches, additional resistance can be incorporated by holding a medicine ball or barbell plate behind your head.

Medicine Ball Leg Lifts

Muscles worked: Lower abdominal region

Exercise type: Single-joint

Movement execution: Lie on your back with your hands clasped behind your head and raise your legs to the vertical position. Place an appropriately weighted medicine ball between your legs just above your knees. Start by lowering your legs under control to just short of the floor, pause briefly, and proceed to lift your legs back up to the vertical position.

Training tips and variations. Younger, less experience trainers may want to use a volleyball or basketball in lieu of a medicine ball for this exercise. Some feel that squeezing the legs together during execution increases the tension on the abdominal muscles.

Volleyball Twists

Muscles worked: Entire abdominal region and obliques

Exercise type: Single-joint

Movement execution: Lie on your back with your knees slightly bent and your feet raised off the floor approximately six inches. Grab a volleyball and hold it at your midsection a few inches above your body. Then, while keeping your knees bent and your legs off the floor, raise your torso up until you're balancing on your tailbone. Proceed to swing from your midsection, keeping your torso as stationary as possible, and touch the ball to the floor. Alternate sides for the required number of repetitions.

Training tips and variations: As you advance, you can replace the volleyball with a medicine ball. To lessen the intensity of the exercise, plant your feet firmly on the ground as opposed to having them in the air.

Side Sit-Ups

Muscles worked: Obliques

Exercise type: Single-joint

Movement execution: Lie on your side and raise your outside leg upward. Then, with your upper hand on the side of your head and your lower arm braced on the floor, crunch sideways toward the raised leg, feeling the oblique contract. Hold briefly at the top, and then return your torso to the floor, leaving your outside leg raised throughout.

Training tips and variations: Side sit-ups are most effective when performed at the end of your workout.

Hanging Leg Raise

Muscles worked: Lower abdominal region

Exercise type: Single-joint

Movement execution: Start by hanging at arm's length from a chinning bar with an overhand grip and your hands approximately shoulder-width apart. Proceed to lift your legs straight in front of you, while keeping your hips and torso as stationary as possible. Hold for a count, and finish by lowering your legs back down to the starting position.

Training tips and variations: Some trainers use grip-enhancing straps when performing hanging leg raises. You can also execute this movement on a vertical bench, where you support yourself by the elbows, thus taking the grip element completely out of the equation.

Floor Back Raise

Muscles worked: Entire lower back region

Exercise type: Single-joint

Movement execution: Lying face down, slowly raise your legs and trunk in unison as high as possible. Hold for a count and lower under control to the starting position.

Training tips and variations: This exercise can be executed on a fitness ball for variety.

Prone Hyperextension

Muscles worked: Entire lower back region

Exercise type: Single-joint

Movement execution: Position yourself so you are face down across a hyperextension bench, with your feet underneath the footpads. With your arms folded across your chest, bend straight down from the waist over the pad. Then, come back up under control until your torso is approximately parallel to the floor.

Training tips and variations: Before training on a hyperextension bench, it is suggested that you first become comfortable with floor back raises. This will ensure that you develop the strength necessary for hyperextension. Resistance can be added to this exercise by holding a barbell plate, dumbbell, or medicine ball across your chest.

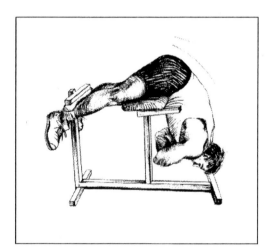 

Good Morning

Muscles worked: Entire lower back region

Exercise type: Single-joint

Movement execution: Standing with your feet close together, hold an appropriately weighted barbell behind your neck. Keeping your legs and back straight, bend at the waist until your upper body is approximately parallel to the floor. Pause briefly, then rise up under control to the standing position.

Training tips and variations: This exercise should be performed with light weights. Some beginners may feel more comfortable executing good mornings with a broomstick instead of a barbell until their strength level increases.

Reverse Back Raise

Muscles worked: Entire lower back region

Exercise type: Single-joint

Movement execution: Lean over a hyperextension bench machine so that the pad supports your midsection and pelvis. (You'll be facing the opposite direction as you would during prone hyperextensions.) Grasp the rollers with your hands, as your legs hang down naturally. Proceed to lift your legs and pelvis in a controlled motion until your legs are slightly higher than your back. Hold for a moment and return to the starting position.

Training tips and variations: Some advanced trainers add resistance to reverse back raises by wearing ankle weights or holding a light dumbbell between their ankles.

Machine Back Extension

Muscles worked: Entire lower back region

Exercise type: Single-joint

Movement execution: Sit comfortably in a lower back machine so that your pelvis is solidly against the back cushion. Proceed to bend backward under control as far as the machine allows. Hold for a count, and then bring yourself back to the starting position.

Training tips and variations: Machine back extensions should always be performed in a deliberate manner. Moving backward too quickly puts you at great risk for injury.

CHAPTER 7

Strength Training Exercises

Upper-Body Exercises

Bench Press

Muscles worked: Middle chest, anterior deltoids, and triceps

Exercise type: Multi-joint

Movement execution: Lying on your back on a flat exercise bench with your hands slightly wider than shoulder width, lift a loaded barbell off the rack and hold it with your arms extended above you. With your feet planted firmly on the ground and your buttocks against the bench, lower the weight under control to your mid-chest. Pause briefly, and proceed to press the bar back up to the locked-out position.

Training tips and variations: It is important to keep your back as flat as possible to the bench during this movement (no arching). Arching your back, while enabling you to lift more weight, takes away from the intent of the exercise and could cause a lower back injury. In addition to using a barbell, the bench press can be performed with dumbbells or on various machines. Using dumbbells allows you to work the chest muscles through a greater range of motion.

Incline Press

Muscles worked: Upper chest, anterior deltoids, and triceps

Exercise type: Multi-joint

Movement execution: Lying on an incline bench (approximately 45-degree incline), take a loaded barbell off the rack. Your grip should be slightly closer than that of the bench press (roughly shoulder width). Lower the weight to your upper chest just below your neck. Pause briefly, and then press the resistance back to the starting position (arms locked).

Training tips and variations: It is important when performing incline presses to avoid the tendency to press the weight out instead of up. Let the position of the bench take care of the direction of the weight, and make sure to lift the resistance straight up on each and every repetition. As with the bench press, this exercise can be executed with dumbbells or machines.

Dip

Muscles worked: Lower chest, anterior deltoids, and triceps

Exercise type: Multi-joint

Movement execution: Start by balancing at arm's length above a dipping bar or parallel bars. Lower yourself under control until your shoulders are slightly above the bars. Then push upward forcefully to the arm's extended position.

Training tips and variations: When performing dips, the farther you lean forward, the more stress you will put on your lower chest. As you move upright, the emphasis goes to your triceps. Some dipping bars allow for varied hand placement. A wider grip exercises your outer chest, while a narrow hand alignment works your inner chest and triceps to a greater degree. Extra resistance can be added to dips by incorporating a weight harness or having a training partner place a dumbbell between your crossed ankles.

Chin-Up

Muscles worked: Upper latissimus dorsi, biceps, and forearms

Exercise type: Multi-joint

Movement execution: Grab hold of a chinning bar with an overhand grip. Your hands should be spaced several inches wider than shoulder-width apart. Pull yourself up so that the bar touches your upper chest. Lower yourself under control to the arms-extended position.

Training tips and variations: When performing conventional chin-ups, arching your back slightly during the concentric (pulling up) portion of the movement is suggested. This action will ensure that you stress your upper back fully. You can do many different types of chin-ups including touching the bar to the back of your neck as opposed to your upper chest, using an underhand grip, or incorporating a double-handled bar. Weight can be added to chin-ups by either a weight harness or having a dumbbell placed between your crossed ankles.

Seated-Cable Row

Muscles worked: Lower latissimus dorsi, posterior deltoids, biceps, and forearms

Exercise type: Multi-joint

Movement execution: Seated in a cable-row apparatus, grip the handle firmly and have your feet supported on the footpad in front of you. With your knees partially bent to protect your lower back, proceed to lower the resistance to the arms-extended position (i.e., the starting point). Then, pull the weight back toward your body, arching your back slightly, and finally touching the handle to your abdomen. Continue by slowly returning the resistance to the starting position.

Training tips and variations: To get the most out of seated-cable rows, it is important to execute the negative phase (lowering the weight) in a controlled fashion. This will stimulate your back muscles fully.

 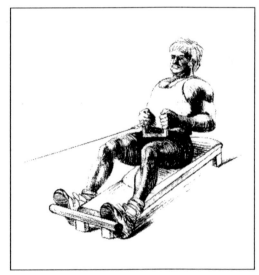

Pulldown

Muscles worked: Upper latissimus dorsi, biceps, and forearms

Exercise type: Multi-joint

Movement Execution: Using a lat machine, grab the bar with a fairly wide, overhand grip. Then, arching your back slightly, pull the bar down until it touches the top of your chest. Pause briefly, and proceed to extend your arms back to the starting position.

Training tips and variations: Similar to chin-ups, it is possible to use a variety of hand placements when performing pulldowns. Unlike chin-ups, because you can exercise with less than your own body weight, additional repetitions can be performed.

One-Arm Dumbbell Row

Muscles worked: Middle and lower latissimus dorsi, biceps, and forearms

Exercise type: Multi-joint

Movement execution: Place one hand and one knee on a flat exercise bench. Grab a sufficiently heavy dumbbell from the floor and, keeping your back flat, lift the weight up to your side. Squeeze your back muscles at the top, and proceed to lower the resistance under control back to the floor.

Training tips and variations: Of all back exercises, the one-arm dumbbell row gives you the opportunity to test your strength. Because your lower back is totally supported, it is possible to use very heavy weights without fear of injury. For variety, this movement can be executed with a cable, using a floor-level pulley. You can do single-arm rows with certain machines, too.

Shoulder Press

Muscles worked: Anterior deltoids, medial deltoids, and triceps

Exercise type: Multi-joint

Movement execution: Seated on a flat exercise bench, grab a loaded barbell off the rack with a slightly wider than shoulder-width grip, and lower it down behind your neck (starting position). Press the weight straight up to the arms-extended position, and lower it slowly back to the starting position.

Training tips and variations: Make sure to warm up your entire shoulder griddle prior to performing shoulder presses. This movement creates a good deal of tension to the shoulder and neck area, so if the muscles are not prepared properly, injury can easily occur. Dumbbells can be substituted for a barbell when executing shoulder presses, as can a variety of exercise machines. Mixing up the way you perform this movement is suggested.

Lateral Raise

Muscles worked: Medial deltoids

Exercise type: Single-joint

Exercise execution: Standing with your knees slightly flexed, take hold of two moderately weighted dumbbells and hold them at your sides. Raise the weights with slightly bent elbows in unison away from your sides, as if you were pouring a pitcher of water, until your arms are just above parallel to the ground. Lower the dumbbells slowly, consciously resisting the weight on the way down.

Training tips and variations: For best results, lateral raises should be performed with moderate to light weights. This movement can be executed seated or on a variety of machines.

Upright Row

Muscles worked: Trapezius, medial deltoids, posterior deltoids, biceps, and forearms

Exercise type: Multi-joint

Movement execution: In a standing position, grasp a loaded barbell with an overhand grip. Your hands should be between five to eight inches apart. Starting with your arms extended, lift the resistance straight up, with the bar as close to your body as possible, to a point just below your chin. Pause briefly, and then lower the barbell under control back to the starting position.

Training tips and variations: To involve more of the deltoids when performing upright rows, widen your grip. To exercise the trapezius more fully, narrow your grip. This exercise can be executed with a floor pulley for variety.

Bent Lateral Raise

Muscles worked: Posterior deltoids

Exercise type: Single-joint

Movement execution: Seated near the end of a flat exercise bench, lean over at the waist and grab two fairly light dumbbells from the floor. Keeping your body balanced, lift the weights out to either side, turning your wrists so that your thumbs are pointed downward. Your arms will be slightly bent throughout, and the weights should be lifted to just above head height before returning to the starting position.

Training tips and variations: For best results, bent laterals should be performed with light weights. The key is to execute the movement in a strict fashion and try to focus on exercising the rear deltoids fully. Bent lateral raises can be done standing, lying prone over an incline bench, or on a variety of machines.

Shoulder Shrug

Muscles worked: Trapezius

Exercise type: Single-joint

Movement execution: Grasp a loaded barbell off a waist-high rack with an overhand, shoulder-width grip. Step away from the rack, holding the barbell with your arms extended and your knees flexed. Keeping your arms extended, shrug your shoulders (i.e., attempt to touch your shoulders to your ears). Pause at the top, and then lower your shoulders slowly back to the starting point.

Training tips and variations: Because of the heavy weight needed to stimulate the trapezius muscles, it is essential that your knees are sufficiently flexed during this movement. Not doing so could cause a lower back injury. Shrugs can also be executed with dumbbells for variety.

Barbell Curl

Muscles worked: Biceps

Exercise type: Single-joint

Movement execution: Standing with your knees slightly bent, grasp a loaded barbell off a waist-high rack with an underhand grip of approximately shoulder width. Let the bar hang down with your arms straight, and then curl the weight up smoothly to the upper chest, keeping your back straight and your elbows close to your torso. Pause at the top, feel the biceps contract, and proceed to lower the resistance in a controlled fashion back to the starting position.

Training tips and variations: To squeeze out a few extra repetitions, a small amount of body swing is acceptable. A floor pulley or dumbbells can be used for this exercise from time to time. However, the barbell version is by far the best for building size and strength in the biceps.

Incline Curl

Muscles worked: Upper biceps

Exercise type: Single-joint

Movement execution: Seated on an incline bench, hold a dumbbell in each hand with your arms fully extended and your palms facing each other. With your elbows in, curl both dumbbells in unison, while slowly twisting your palms upward, to your front deltoids. Then, lower the weights slowly back to the starting position.

Training tips and variations: It is important that you pause at the bottom of the movement to prevent yourself from using momentum for the next repetition. The dumbbells can be lifted one at a time for variety.

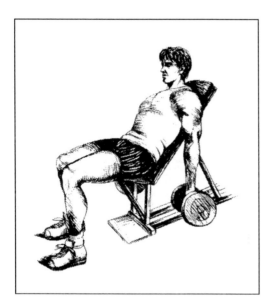 

Preacher Curl

Muscles worked: Lower biceps

Exercise type: Single-joint

Movement execution: Seated on a preacher bench with your chest against the pad, grasp a barbell with an underhand grip from the rack. Your arms should be approximately shoulder-width apart. Without rocking backward, curl the bar up so that your biceps are fully contracted. Pause at the top, and then lower the bar slowly back to the arms-extended position.

Training tips and variations: Some trainers like to reverse their grip to overhand when performing preacher curls. This brings the forearms into play to a greater degree. For variety, dumbbells or various machines can be used for preacher curls.

Triceps Press-Down

Muscles worked: Triceps

Exercise type: Single-joint

Movement execution: Grasp a short bar from an overhead pulley with an overhand grip and your hands six to eight inches apart. With your elbows close to your torso and your knees slightly flexed, push the bar down, locking your arms at the bottom. Release, and then bring the resistance back to the starting point (approximately mid-chest height) before repeating.

Training tips and variations: It is important not to move your torso forward during the execution of triceps press-downs. This will take considerable stress off your arms. For variety, you can used a different shaped bar, a specially designed rope, or a lat machine. Also, you can experiment with hand placement or even incorporate an underhand grip for added stretch.

Lying Triceps Extension

Muscles worked: Triceps

Exercise type: Single-joint

Movement execution: Lying on a flat exercise bench with your head just off the edge, take hold of a barbell with a slightly closer than shoulder-width grip and place it just above your forehead. Keeping your elbows stationary, push the resistance up by extending your arms to the locked-out position. Then, lower the bar slowly back to the starting position.

Training tips and variations: Many trainers feel that using an E-Z curl bar (a specially shaped bar that allows for increased grip stability) when performing lying triceps extensions gives more control and a slightly increased range of motion. If you do not have access to a bench, it is possible to do this exercise while lying on the floor.

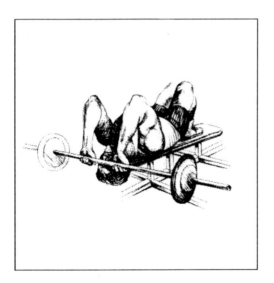 

Seated Triceps Extension

Muscles worked: Triceps

Exercise type: Single-joint

Movement execution: Sit on the end of a flat exercise bench and grasp a barbell overhead with your hands 10 to 12 inches apart. Bring the weight behind your head until your upper arms are parallel to the floor (starting position). Then, extend your arms, pushing the bar overhead to the locked-out position.

Training tips and variations: Some trainers prefer to perform this movement standing as opposed to sitting. Dumbbells, an E-Z curl bar, or an extension machine can be used for variety.

Lower-Body Exercises

Squat

Muscles worked: Hips, quadriceps, buttocks, hamstrings, and lower back

Exercise type: Multi-joint

Movement execution: Standing with your feet approximately shoulder-width apart and pointed slightly outward, rest a loaded barbell across your shoulders behind your neck. With your hands balancing the bar, bend your knees and lower yourself until your thighs are just below parallel to the floor. Keeping your head up and your back straight, drive yourself back to the standing position.

Training tips and variations: When performing squats, it is important to keep your knees behind the front of your feet throughout the movement. Not doing so creates extra stress on the knee joints. Also, if you've never squatted before, it is advisable to use light weight until you feel comfortable with the movement. A number of machines are available that simulate the barbell squat. Dumbbells can also be used periodically for variety.

Leg Press

Muscles worked: Quadriceps, hips, buttocks, and hamstrings

Exercise type: Multi-joint

Movement execution: Seated in a leg-press machine, place your feet near the top of the foot piece, with your toes pointed slightly outward and your legs approximately shoulder-width apart. Unlock the weight and bend your knees, lowering the resistance as far as possible. Press the weight back up through your heels to just short of the leg-extended position.

Training tips and variations: As mentioned in the movement execution, it is suggested that you do not lock your knees at the top of the leg press. This strategy allows you to maintain tension on your thighs throughout the movement. A variety of leg-press machines are available for your use. The same training principles apply to all.

Lunge

Muscles worked: Quadriceps, buttocks, hips, hamstrings, and calves

Exercise type: Multi-joint

Movement execution: Standing upright holding a barbell across your shoulders behind your neck, step forward, bend at the knees, and bring your rear knee close to the floor. Then, proceed by driving yourself powerfully back to the standing position.

Training tips and variations: Lunges can be performed by alternating legs every repetition or by doing separate sets for each leg. Separate-leg sets work the leg muscles more intensely and are suggested. Dumbbells held at your sides can also be used for lunges. Athletes with a history of knee problems should avoid lunges.

Front Squat

Muscles worked: Quadriceps, hips, buttocks, hamstrings, and lower back

Exercise type: Multi-joint

Movement execution: Place a loaded barbell at chest height on a rack. Step under the rack, and position the bar across the front of your shoulders with your hands balancing the resistance. Your elbows should be rotated so that they are ahead of the bar. Step away from the rack and proceed to bend your knees, keeping your head up and back straight, and lower yourself until your upper legs are below parallel to the floor. Pause briefly, and explode upward to the starting position.

Training tips and variations: Some trainers prefer to cross their arms in front of their shoulders with their hands placed on top of the bar when executing front squats. This exercise can be performed with dumbbells for variety. However, the barbell version of the front squat is far superior for strength development.

Straight-Legged Dead Lift

Muscles worked: Hamstrings and lower back

Exercise type: Multi-joint

Movement execution: Standing, take hold of a barbell with an overhand, shoulder-width grip. Keeping your legs straight, bend at the waist with your back straight and your arms extended. Pause momentarily when your torso is parallel to the floor, and then straighten slowly back to the standing position.

Training tips and variations: It is best to perform straight-legged dead lifts in a deliberate manner, especially when incorporating heavy weights. Dumbbells or a floor pulley can be used in lieu of a barbell periodically for this exercise.

Step-Up

Muscles worked: Hips, quadriceps, buttocks, and calves

Exercise type: Multi-joint

Movement execution: With a barbell resting across your shoulders and your hands balancing the resistance, step up on to a box (the height of the box can vary depending on your stature, strength level, and objectives) as if you were climbing stairs. Pause at the top with your legs straight, and then step down carefully back to the floor.

Training tips and variations: Step-ups can be performed either by alternating legs every repetition or by doing one complete set with your left leg, followed by one complete set with your right leg. For variety, dumbbells held at your sides can be used instead of a barbell.

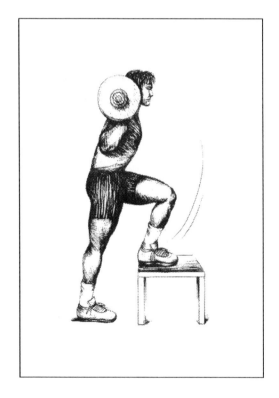 

Leg Extension

Muscles worked: Quadriceps

Exercise type: Single-joint

Movement execution: Using a leg-extension machine, sit and anchor your feet under the cushions. Then, extend your lower legs up as high as possible and hold for a count. Lower the weight under control to the starting point.

Training tips and variations: Leg extensions can be executed one leg at a time for variety.

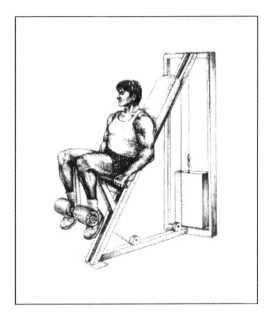 

Leg Curl

Muscles worked: Hamstrings

Exercise type: Single-joint

Movement execution: Lying on your stomach on a leg-curl machine, place your heels under the pads. Proceed by pulling your heels up as close as possible to your buttocks, while keeping your body flat on the machine. Pause at the top, and lower the resistance back to the starting position.

Training tips and variations: As with leg extensions, you can train one leg at a time when performing leg curls. In addition to the conventional leg curl machine, some gyms have equipment that allows you to isolate one leg at a time from a standing position.

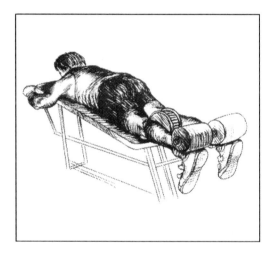 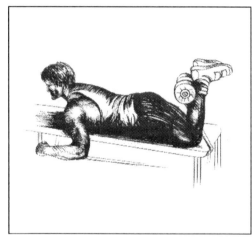

Standing Calf Raise

Muscles worked: Calves

Exercise type: Single-joint

Movement execution: Stand with your toes on a block or a step with a barbell resting comfortably across the back of your shoulders. Your hands should hold the resistance in place. Proceed by lowering your heels as far as you can toward the ground, maintaining slightly flexed knees throughout. When you reach a fully stretched position, come up on your toes as high up as possible.

Training tips and variations: Since calves are involved in almost every athletic activity (running, jumping, sliding, etc.), they develop quite a high tolerance for training. Therefore, this stubborn muscle group must be trained with heavy weights. You can choose from a variety of standing calf-raise machines in lieu of a barbell. Dumbbells held in each hand can also be utilized for standing calf raises.

Combination Exercises

Combination exercises work a variety of muscles in unison. They are meant to be performed at a high rate of speed. Before incorporating combination lifts into your workout schedule, a solid base of overall body strength must be attained. Therefore, these movements will not be employed until cycle three of your year-round strength program. Additionally, because of the complicated and intense nature of combination lifts, proper form is critical for success and injury prevention.

Push Press

Muscles worked: Upper chest, anterior deltoids, quadriceps, hips, lower back, and triceps

Exercise type: Multi-joint

Movement execution: In a standing position, grab a barbell off a chest-high rack with a shoulder-width grip and rest it on your upper chest just below your neck. Start by bending your knees approximately halfway to parallel, and then simultaneously straighten your legs and push the weight straight up overhead to the arms-extended position. Lower slowly back to the starting position and repeat.

Training tips and variations: During the positive (lifting) phase of the push press, make sure to keep your body positioned under the weight throughout the movement. Not doing so could cause a loss of balance and possible injury. Dumbbells can be used for this exercise, but tend to be somewhat awkward.

High Pull

Muscles worked: Hips, quadriceps, lower back, calves, trapezius, medial deltoids, posterior deltoids, biceps, and forearms

Movement type: Multi-joint

Movement execution: With an overhand, shoulder-width grip, grab a barbell off a waist-high rack and position it on your lower thighs just above your knees. Your back should be flat, your head straight, your knees flexed, and your feet hip-width apart. Proceed to explosively move the resistance upward by pulling with your arms and shrugging with your shoulders until the bar is just below your chin. The bar should remain close to your body throughout. Your calves will raise up in tandem with the path of the bar. Lower the bar to the starting position.

Training tips and variations: You always want to keep your shoulders over the bar when executing high pulls. Dumbbells can be used in place of a barbell for this exercise, but similar to push presses, the barbell version is most effective.

Hang Clean

Muscles worked: Hips, quadriceps, lower back, calves, anterior deltoids, medial deltoids, forearms, and biceps

Exercise type: Multi-joint

Movement execution: Assume the same hand position (overhand, shoulder-width grip) and starting position (bar resting on your lower thighs) as you would when executing a high pull. Your back should be flat, your head straight, your knees comfortable flexed, and your feet at hip-width apart. Proceed to extend your hips up and slightly forward, moving to the balls of your feet while shrugging your shoulders. Move under the bar, elevating your feet momentarily, and, while rotating your elbows, receive the bar on your anterior deltoids. Make sure your knees and hips are sufficiently bent to absorb the resistance.

Training tips and variations: Most beginners should perfect their form by using a lighter object such as a broomstick for hang cleans.

Explosive Squats

Muscles worked: Hips, quadriceps, buttocks, lower back, and calves

Exercise type: Multi-joint

Movement execution: As with the conventional squat, stand with your feet approximately shoulder-width apart and pointed slightly outward and rest a loaded barbell across your shoulders. With your hands balancing the resistance, bend your knees and lower yourself so that your thighs are just below parallel to the floor. Keeping your head up and your back straight, explode powerfully up to the standing position, ending as high up as possible on your toes. Lower to the flatfooted position, pause briefly, and repeat.

Training tips and variations: Although explosive squats are meant to be performed at a high rate of speed, it is still a priority that you maintain proper lifting form. Periodically dumbbells can be used instead of a barbell for this movement.

CHAPTER 8

Year-Round Strength Training for Volleyball

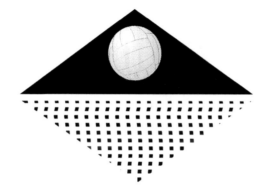

Designing a year-round strength training program for volleyball is extremely challenging. Tremendous demands come with participating in competitive volleyball, and finding the time, energy, and motivation to build and maintain strength on a year-round basis takes *considerable planning and effort.*

The basic premise of a volleyball player's strength program is relatively simple to explain, but unfortunately very difficult to achieve. Athletes must endeavor to reach peak levels of strength on the initial day of organized practice, and maintain that strength over the course of an entire volleyball season. No easy task to say the least.

Year-Round Program

A volleyball player's yearly strength program should consist of *six separate training cycles*. Cycling is based on incorporating a variety of exercises, weights, set sequences, repetition schemes, and training intensities within a given training year. This proven approach is designed to boost an athlete's strength level in a safe and progressive manner.

The strength workouts themselves will be split into three sections in the off-season and two during the competitive season. Off-season workout #1 focuses on the lower body and core. Off-season workout #2 will consist of exercises for the upper body and midsection. And off-season workout #3 features combination movements such as hang cleans and push presses that exercise both the upper and lower body in unison.

During the regular campaign, two different full-body strength workouts will be incorporated, one emphasizing the lower body and core, and the other focusing on the upper body. Strength workouts should take place on three non-consecutive days per week in the off-season and a minimum of two days per week during the competitive season. Examples of individual workouts for all six cycles are outlined in the following sections. In addition, the duration of each cycle, training loads, repetition schemes, and training objectives are discussed.

Core Cycle

Cycle #1

Duration: Three weeks

Load: Light

Repetition Scheme: 15-50

Objective: This short, three-week cycle focuses on building a base of strength in both the lower back and midsection. As mentioned in the section on core training, lower back and abdominal strength are crucial to not only on-court volleyball performance but weight room effectiveness as well. Getting a head start on training these important muscle groups will start your year-round strength program off on the right foot.

Exercise:	Sets and Repetitions:
Floor Back Raise	4 x 20
Bench Crunch	4 x 50
Good Morning	3 x 15
Leg-in-the-Air Sit-Up	3 x 50
Side Sit-Up	2 x 50 (each side)
Total Sets: 16	

Table 8-1. Sample cycle #1 core workout

Exercise:	Sets and Repetitions:
Prone Hyperextension	4 x 15
Medicine Ball Leg Lift	4 x 20
Reverse Back Raise	3 x 15
Volleyball Twist	3 x 25
Twisting Sit-Up	2 x 50 (each side)
Total Sets: 16	

Table 8-2. Sample cycle #1 core workout

Exercise:	Sets and Repetitions:
Good Morning	4 x 15
Hanging Leg Raise	4 x 20
Machine Back Extension	3 x 20
Crunch	3 x 50
Side Sit-Up	2 x 50 (each side)
Total Sets: 16	

Table 8-3. Sample cycle #1 core workout

Off-Season Cycles

Cycle #2

Duration: Four weeks

Load: Light

Repetition Scheme: 12-15

Objective: Cycle #2 is the acclamation stage. It is the time to become accustomed to progressive resistance training again. Or, if you've never strength trained before, becoming familiar with the basics of working out with weights. Perfecting exercise form is a priority for cycle #2. Making a habit of using correct lifting technique early in your program will go a long way toward ensuring a successful strength training year. Remember, bad lifting habits are like comfortable chairs: easy to fall into, hard to get out of. During the last week of this training cycle, you should have a good feel for your strength level, using a 12-repetition maximum on all multi-joint lifts.

Exercise:	Sets and Repetitions:
Incline Press	1 x 15, 1 x 12, 1 x 15
Pulldown	1 x 15, 1 x 12, 1 x 15
Shoulder Press	3 x 12
Dip	2 x 12
Bent Lateral Raise	1 x 15, 1 x 12, 1 x 15
Barbell Curl	3 x 15
Volleyball Twist	3 x 25
Hanging Leg Raise	3 x 20
Total Sets: 23	

Table 8-4. Sample cycle #2 upper-body workout

Exercise:	Sets and Repetitions:
Leg Press	1 x 15, 2 x 12, 1 x 15
Straight-Legged Dead Lift	3 x 15
Leg Extension	3 x 15
Standing Calf Raise	3 x 15
Prone Hyperextension	3 x 15
Volleyball Twist	4 x 25
Total Sets: 20	

Table 8-5. Sample cycle #2 lower-body workout

Cycle #3

Duration: Six weeks

Load: Medium

Repetition Scheme: 8-12

Objective: By this time, you should be thoroughly familiar with all of the upper body, lower body, and core movements in your program. Developing a solid base of overall body strength is the goal of cycle #3. This cycle also introduces you to combination movements such as hang cleans and push presses. These exercises will be incorporated slowly over a number of workouts during this cycle, with the emphasis on learning correct execution. As you become more comfortable with combination lifts more weight can gradually be added to the bar.

Exercise:	Sets and Repetitions:
Chin-Up	1 x 12, 2 x 10, 1 x 12
Bench Press	1 x 12, 2 x 8, 1 x 10
Upright Row	1 x 12, 1 x 10, 1 x 12
Lateral Raise	3 x 12
Lying Triceps Extension	3 x 10
Preacher Curl	3 x 12
Medicine Ball Leg Lift	3 x 25
Side Sit-Up	3 x 50 (each side)
Total Sets: 23	

Table 8-6. Sample cycle #3 upper-body workout

Exercise:	Sets and Repetitions:
Squat	1 x 12, 1 x 10, 1 x 8, 1 x 12
Leg Curl	3 x 12
Lunge	1 x 12, 1 x 10, 1 x 12
Standing Calf Raise	3 x 12
Good Morning	3 x 12
Twisting Sit-Up	4 x 25 (each side)
Total Sets: 20	

Table 8-7. Sample cycle #3 lower-body workout

Exercise:	Sets and Repetitions:
High Pull	1 x 12, 3 x 8, 1 x 12
Explosive Squat	1 x 12, 3 x 10, 1 x 12
Hang Clean	1 x 12, 1 x 10, 2 x 8, 1 x 12
Total Sets: 15	

Table 8-8. Sample cycle #3 combination workout

Cycle #4

Duration: Six weeks

Load: Medium/Heavy

Repetition Scheme: 6-10

Objective: During this cycle intensity should be ramped up considerably. Longer rest periods between sets should be employed, and strength gains become your priority for all lifts (upper body, lower body, and combination). By the conclusion of cycle #4, you should be well on your way to reaching your full strength potential. Although you will be lifting heavier weights, it is still critical that you maintain proper exercise form. Remember that poor execution will not only slow your strength progression but will also inevitably lead to injury.

Exercise:	Sets and Repetitions:
DB Incline Press	1 x 10, 1 x 8, 1 x 6, 1 x 8
Pulley Row	1 x 10, 2 x 8, 1 x 10
Shoulder Press	1 x 8, 1 x 6, 1 x 8
Triceps Press-Down	1 x 10, 1 x 8, 1 x 10
Incline Curl	1 x 10, 1 x 8, 1 x 10
Leg-in-the-Air Sit-Up	3 x 50
Volleyball Twist	2 x 50 (each side)
Total Sets: 22	

Table 8-9. Sample cycle #4 upper-body workout

Exercise:	Sets and Repetitions:
Step-Up	1 x 10, 1 x 8, 1 x 6, 1 x 8
Straight-Legged Dead Lift	1 x 10, 1 x 8, 1 x 6, 1 x 10
Lunge	3 x 8
Reverse Back Raise	3 x 10
Standing Calf Raise	3 x 10
Crunch	3 x 50
Total Sets: 20	

Table 8-10. Sample cycle #4 lower-body workout

Exercise:	Sets and Repetitions:
Push Press	1 x 10, 1 x 8, 2 x 6, 1 x 8
Hang Clean	1 x 10, 1 x 8, 2 x 6, 1 x 10
Explosive Squat	1 x 10, 3 x 8, 1 x 10
Total Sets: 15	

Table 8-11. Sample cycle #4 combination workout

Cycle #5

Duration: Five weeks

Load: Heavy

Repetition Scheme: 4-6

Objective: Reaching maximum strength is the goal of this final off-season training cycle. Combination movements will play a bigger role in cycle #5 with every other training session being a combination workout. Excitement should be high at this time of year, as the competitive season looms ever closer. And although you won't be spending as much time in the weight room as in previous cycles due to volleyball skill work and sports specific conditioning taking precedence, strength gains are still possible and should be the objective. At the conclusion of this five-week period you should be at your strongest in all lifts.

Exercise:	Sets and Repetitions:
One-Arm Dumbbell Row	1 x 6, 2 x 5, 1 x 6
Bench Press	1 x 6, 2 x 4, 1 x 5
Shoulder Shrug	3 x 6
Bent Lateral Raise	2 x 6
Hammer Curl	2 x 6
Seated Triceps Extension	2 x 6
Hanging Leg Raise	3 x 25
Side Sit-Up	2 x 50 (each side)
Total Sets: 22	

Table 8-12. Sample cycle #5 upper-body workout

Exercise:	Sets and Repetitions:
Front Squat	1 x 6, 2 x 4, 1 x 6
Leg Curl	3 x 6
Leg Extension	3 x 6
Good Morning	3 x 6
Standing Calf Raise	3 x 6
Medicine Ball Leg Lift	4 x 25
Total Sets: 20	

Table 8-13. Sample cycle #5 lower-body workout

Exercise:	Sets and Repetitions:
Hang Clean	1 x 6, 1 x 5, 1 x 4, 1 x 5, 1 x 6
Push Press	3 x 6
High Pull	1 x 6, 1 x 5, 1 x 4, 2 x 6
Total Sets: 13	

Table 8-14. Sample cycle #5 combination workout

In-Season Cycle

Cycle #6

Duration: Throughout the entire competitive season

Load: Medium

Repetition Scheme: 8-12

Objective: The goal of in-season strength training for volleyball can be described in one word: maintenance. Because of games, practices, team meetings and film sessions, travel, school, along with all the of other obligations and responsibilities in your life, it is virtually impossible to make gains in strength during this time of year. But with a strong commitment and skillful time management, you can preserve the strength you've developed in the off-season. Most volleyball players, and athletes in general regardless of which sport, become somewhat deconditioned during a long, grueling season. Adhering to the strength training protocol prescribed in this chapter can help you reverse this process, and will enable you to sustain peak levels of strength, conditioning, and performance throughout the competitive season. The following examples outline some suggestions that you can adopt to help you maintain strength all season long:

- *Use multi-joint exercises*: Although combination movements are not prescribed for in-season use by volleyball players, other multi-joint exercises such as squats, incline presses, and upright rows will be the staples of your in-season routine. As previously mentioned, using multi-joint lifts is the most energy and time efficient way to strength train since these movements work a number of muscles at once.

- *Strength train immediately following matches*: If you have access to the appropriate facilities, strength training immediately after matches is a fantastic way to keep current with your routine. Working out after matches also helps cool your body down after intense exertion. Post-match strength workouts should be brief (no longer than 30 minutes), and large amounts of hydrating fluids must be consumed before, during, and after the training session. It is imperative that you respect your energy level after competition, along with monitoring any injuries you may have sustained during the match that may make strength training unadvisable.

- *Use off days constructively*: As any athlete can attest, off days during the competitive season are precious commodities. A free day provides a volleyball player with an excellent opportunity to hit the weights hard. If you're lucky enough to have a four- or five-day break during the regular season, by all means take full advantage of it in the weight room. This time will not only help you maintain your strength, but it will energize you for the rest of the competitive campaign. So if you have the energy and do not have a match the following day, plan on strength training hard on your off days.

- *Schedule a team-strength workout instead of practice*: It is ultimately up to the coach of course, but having a team strength training session, in lieu of practice, can accomplish a great deal. Along with allowing players to stay up with their programs, it provides everyone—players, coaches, trainers, and even team managers—a mental break from the monotony of regular practice.

- *Strength train consistently in the off-season*: Perhaps the best way to ensure that you remain strong throughout the long volleyball season is to commit yourself to working consistently hard in the weight room in the off-season. The more strength you build in the off-season, the easier it will be to maintain peak performance levels when it counts during the competitive season.

Exercise:	Sets and Repetitions:
Lunge	1 x 12, 1 x 10, 1 x 12
Straight-Legged Dead Lift	1 x 12, 1 x 10, 1 x 12
Incline Press	1 x 10, 1 x 8, 1 x 10
Pulldown	1 x 12, 1 x 8, 1 x 10
Upright Row	3 x 10
Reverse Back Raise	3 x 12
Crunch	4 x 50
Total Sets: 22	

Table 8-15. Sample cycle #6 full body workout

Exercise:	Sets and Repetitions:
Squat	1 x 12, 1 x 10, 1 x 8, 1 x 10
Step-Up	2 x 10
Chin-Up	1 x 12, 1 x 8, 1 x 10
Bench Press	1 x 10, 1 x 8, 1 x 10
Shoulder Press	1 x 10, 1 x 8, 1 x 12
Machine Back Extension	3 x 12
Hanging Leg Raise	3 x 25
Total Sets: 21	

Table 8-16. Sample cycle #6 full body workout

PART IV
MOVEMENT TRAINING FOR VOLLEYBALL

CHAPTER 9

Balance Training

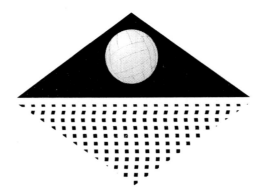

Whether you are shooting a basketball, pitching a baseball, or serving a volleyball, balancing your body under its center of gravity is a prerequisite for success. Possessing *good balance* is essential for volleyball players. Every aspect of the sport from digging a hard driven ball to blocking a strong spike requires that athletes be on balance ready to respond at a moment's notice. Remember, balance must always come before any forceful movement, whether it be jumping, sprinting, or sliding.

While some athletes possess naturally better balance than others, it is an attribute that can be developed and greatly improved with hard work and perseverance. Unfortunately, many volleyball players neglect direct balance training either because they haven't been exposed to it or feel that the combination of playing volleyball itself and engaging in other conditioning disciplines (running, agility training, plyometrics, etc.) makes balance work unnecessary and redundant.

Avoiding balance training, regardless of the reason, is a mistake. Direct balance exercises strengthen small stabilizing muscles of the lower body that are usually not worked otherwise, and performing them on a consistent basis will contribute greatly toward you becoming a more athletic and better overall volleyball player.

Equipment

- *Tape*: Tape is used for *line-touch* drills. Any type of athletic tape is fine as long as the color contrasts with the training surface.

- *Medicine balls*: Medicine balls have long been used in the strength and conditioning community for balance enhancement. The weight of the ball will vary depending upon an athlete's strength level and the particular exercise involved. For most balance drills, incorporating between a three-kilogram (6.6 pounds) and five-kilogram (11 pounds) medicine ball is suggested.

- *Balance pad*: A balance pad is simply a foam mat that causes an athlete's feet to sink into the cushion, thus creating instability.

- *Balance board*: A variety of balance boards are available today. Most consist of a single platform with a fulcrum (or fulcrums) underneath that creates an unstable environment that forces the athlete to constantly adjust to maintain balance. Think of a standing on the middle of a seesaw, and you'll get the basic idea how a balance board works. Some balance boards move in three axes for greater instability. You can perform numerous balance exercises on this equipment, a few of which are detailed later in this chapter.

- *Footwear*: Many strength and conditioning specialists feel that balance training, especially when undertaken on a balance pad or balance board, should be done barefoot. This will help to strengthen your feet and ankles to a greater degree. Of course, if you're training on a rough surface or have any type of lower leg or foot injury, wearing sneakers or the appropriate training shoes during balance workouts is recommended.

Parameters of Balance Training

All balance exercises in the following program will be performed *unilaterally* (on one leg). They progress from simple (single-leg stands) to advanced (balance board medicine ball pick-ups). The movements should be executed in a smooth, controlled manner while standing on the ball of your foot. Training balance in a herky-jerky style or from a flatfooted position defeats the purpose of the exercise. Balance work is best accomplished either after lower- body strength sessions, agility/plyometric workouts, or volleyball activities.

As mentioned previously, some athletes have naturally better balance than others, so it is important to move through the exercises at your own pace. Many of the exercises are much more difficult than they appear. Don't get frustrated. With time, improvements in exercise execution and overall balance will come.

Schedule Description

Program Length

A balance-training program for volleyball should be a *year-round endeavor*, with the exception of training breaks where complete abstinence from exercise is scheduled. Unlike plyometrics or intense agility training, direct balance work involves no impact or hard pounding to the ground, making it easy on the body with a very low injury risk. Therefore, balance training can be implemented on a year-round basis.

Number of Workouts Per Week

Two direct balance workouts per week are suggested in the off-season. During the season, one session per week is sufficient.

Sets and Repetitions

Eight to twelve total sets per workout are recommended for balance training. One set in balance-training terminology will include performing the exercise on each leg. Usually the sets will be spread among three to five different balance movements. The repetition range per set will be between 10 and 15 for each leg, depending on the particular exercise involved and the strength level of the athlete.

Rest Between Sets

The rest between sets of balance exercises will vary between 30 and 90 seconds. Of course, much will depend on the intensity of the effort. For example, a set of single-leg stands will require much less recovery time than will a set of balance board medicine ball pick-ups using a five-kilogram medicine ball.

Workout Duration

Most balance workouts can be completed in less than 20 minutes.

Balance Exercises

- *Single-leg stands*: This simple exercise entails standing erect on one leg with your knee slightly flexed for 30 to 60 seconds. The raised leg should be bent at the knee and placed behind you parallel to the floor. One-legged stands are usually reserved for young or beginning volleyball players, but they can be incorporated as a warm-up for more advanced trainers or for athletes coming off leg injuries. It is best to perform this exercise on a balance pad.

- *Line touches*: Place a strip of tape on the floor in front of you. Stand on one leg where the tape starts and, with your back straight, proceed to bend at the hips, knee, and ankle, reaching as far as you can with the hand of the raised leg and touch the tape. Continue for the required number of repetitions and then repeat with the opposite leg. Make sure to mark your results from week to week to check improvement.

Single-leg stands

Line touches

- *Around the worlds*: Standing on your right leg with your hips, knee, and ankle slightly flexed, move a volleyball as fast as possible under your knee from right to left, then around your back from left to right. Reverse directions (right to left around your back; left to right under your knee) and continue alternating for the required number of repetitions. Stand on your left leg and repeat the action. As you progress and improve balance, substitute the volleyball with a three-kilogram medicine ball. Advanced athletes can try this exercise on a balance pad or balance board.

- *Medicine ball pick-ups*: Place an appropriately weighted medicine ball approximately a foot in front of you. Begin by standing on one leg with your knee slightly flexed. Bend forward at the hips, knee, and ankle and with two hands grab the ball from the floor and return to the standing position. You can either bring the ball up to your midsection or, to increase the difficulty, raise it overhead. After completing the repetition hand the ball to your training partner and have him place it back on the floor. Continue for the required number of repetitions. Then switch legs and repeat.

  To make the exercise more challenging, place the ball further away from you. This forces you to bend down lower, which will contribute to building additional strength and balance. Advanced trainers may want to try this exercise while standing on a balance board. Not only will the instability of the board make the movement more difficult, but you'll be required to go below *floor level* to pick up the ball, which increases the tension on your lower back, hamstrings, and buttocks. When performing medicine ball pick-ups, it is always a good idea to have a stationary object (person, wall, weight machine, etc.) at your side to grab hold of if balance is lost.

Around the worlds

Medicine ball pick-ups

- *One-legged side toss and catch*: Stand on one leg with your grounded knee slightly flexed and face forward. Begin by twisting your torso as far as you can to the left while keeping your grounded leg stationary and receive a medicine ball pass from your training partner, who will be standing five to eight feet away off your left shoulder. Once you catch the pass, immediately position the ball just above waist height, 8 to 12 inches from your body. From there, twist your torso as far as possible to your right, keeping your arms and grounded leg stationary. Then in a controlled but forceful manner, swing back in the opposite direction and release the ball just after it crosses the middle of your body to your training partner. Continue for the required number of repetitions. Do the same from the opposite side.

  As with medicine ball pick-ups, advanced trainers can increase the difficulty by standing on a balance board during execution. Beginners may be more comfortable using a volleyball instead of a medicine ball for this exercise.

Exercise:	Sets and Repetitions:
Single-Leg Stands	2 x 60 seconds
Line Touches	2 x 15
Around the Worlds	2 x 10
Medicine Ball Pick-Ups	1 x 12, 1 x 15, 1 x 12
One-Legged Side Toss and Catch	1 x 12, 1 x 15, 1 x 12

Table 9-1. Sample balance workout

CHAPTER 10

Plyometrics

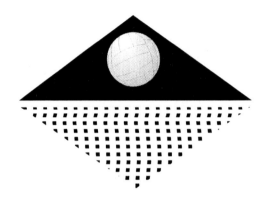

Plyometrics has experienced tremendous popularity over the past decade-and-a-half within the strength and conditioning community. Originally known as *jump training* in Europe, *plyometric training* entails a series of jumps, hops, bounds, and other dynamic athletic movements such as medicine ball throws and explosive push-ups. The exercises are designed to *link speed with strength* to produce power that is accomplished by stretching or loading the muscles as fast as possible prior to a forceful contraction. Perhaps the simplest way to understand how plyometrics works is to think of stretching an elastic band to the point of ultimate tension and then letting it go, allowing the force and energy to move explosively in the opposite direction.

What Volleyball Players Can Expect from Plyometrics

Plyometrics has its share of staunch proponents who feel it is the holy grail of athletic performance-enhancing tools—the *final frontier* of sports conditioning if you will. It also has a smattering of detractors who believe it is basically a well-hyped fraud that will inevitably cause serious injury. While both sides of this argument are a little extreme, the supporters' case has proven to have more validity. In fact, many athletes who compete in explosive-type sports, most prominently track and field competitors, have shown tangible results through the use of plyometrics. Sprinters have lowered times, high jumpers have raised jump heights, and shot putters have increased throwing distances all in the name of plyometric training.

Similar to track and field athletes, volleyball players can benefit substantially from plyometrics. It is perhaps the *best* training method for increasing vertical jumping ability, which of course is of paramount importance to all volleyball athletes. (It has been estimated that over the course of an hour match a player will leave his feet over 70 times.) Plyometric training also enhances off-the-mark quickness, builds overall power and explosiveness, and perfects landing technique, all attributes that will improve on-court performance.

Before you get too carried away with the benefits of plyometrics, this training modality does have some drawbacks and limitations. It will *not*, as some advocates claim, turn a 30-inch vertical jump into a 40-inch vertical jump. Increases of three to five inches are more realistic. You will face some degree of injury risk with plyometrics, especially if engaged in too frequently, executed improperly, or performed by unfit individuals. Because of its intense demands, plyometrics has been known to contribute to overtraining and body breakdown. This as you know can inhibit performance and be a precursor to injury. Volleyball players, because of the constant jumping their sport requires, must be acutely cognizant not to go overboard with plyometric training.

Overall, however, the pluses strongly outweigh the minuses. So it is recommended that all healthy, well-conditioned, and improvement-conscious volleyball players make plyometrics part of their overall conditioning program.

Developing Your Plyometric Training Program

A number of factors should be taken into account when designing a plyometric training program for volleyball, including the following:

Equipment

Although many plyometric drills can be performed without equipment, you should be familiar with a few basic accessories, including:

*   *Barriers*: Barriers are incorporated into many plyometric drills. Their height can vary from as low as six inches to as high as two feet or more, depending on the nature of the drill and the athletic ability of the practitioner. The safest barriers are made of foam padding. The simplest are plastic cones. Obviously, any hard object should never be used as a plyometric barrier.

- *Boxes*: Boxes used for plyometrics must be sturdy, have semi-soft, nonslip landing surfaces, and should range from a few inches to over three feet in height. The top of the box should measure a minimum of 18 by 24 inches. Any less of a landing area would be dangerous. Many fitness stores and most all sports training catalogs sell specialized and adjustable plyometric boxes.

- *Medicine balls*: Medicine balls have come full circle in terms of popularity as a conditioning tool. Originally used exclusively by boxers in their fight preparation, medicine balls are today staples in the training of a variety of athletes from football players to golfers. The balls themselves are weighted spheres that come in an assortment of weights, sizes, and colors. Rubber medicine balls are recommended because they grip easily, bounce evenly when they hit the floor, and are generally safer to use.

- *Weighted vests*: The weighted vest is an outstanding tool for increasing vertical jump. It can be used in a variety of settings—in the weight room when performing step-ups, lunges, and squats; on the beach for executing explosive sand jumps; and on the track, field, or gym floor implementing any number of plyometric exercises. Because the resistance is evenly distributed throughout the upper torso, plyometric training with a weighted vest is not only performance enhancing but relatively safe as well.

  Most vests are weight adjustable, usually in two- to four-pound increments. It is suggested to use the type that comes with the soft beanbag weights as opposed to metal rods. Most sporting goods stores carry a variety of weighted vests as do the majority of sports/fitness catalogs and online sporting goods merchants.

  Maintaining proper jumping form is crucial to successful weighted vest plyometric training. As resistance increases, form tends to suffer. To counteract this and ensure safety, it is best to add weight gradually. Many advanced athletes add only two pounds per week to the vest to allow for maximum strength acclamation. Additionally, the total weight of the vest should never be more than 8 to 10 percent of your body weight.

- *Ankle weights and strength shoes*: As a rule, it is discouraged to use any equipment worn below the knee for plyometric training. Ankle weights and strength shoes fall into this category. Wearing these products or others like them while engaging in intense jumping or movement training does nothing to improve performance and can contribute to aggravating the patella tendon in the front of the knee joint.

- *Other jumping aids*: A number of so-called jump-training aids are on the market today. Most are gimmicks that can be easily replicated without spending top dollar to purchase. The only jump trainer that would be of use to volleyball players is the *Super Vertical Leaper*. This piece of equipment makes use of resistance bands that are attached from the floor to waist and shoulder belts. After securing the belts, the athlete performs a series of explosive vertical jumps, concentrating on popping up quickly after landing. The *Super Vertical Leaper* distributes force equally between shoulder and waist, allowing for maximum safety and effect. Sporting good stores probably won't carry the *Super Vertical Leaper*, but you should be able to order it though the majority of sports/fitness catalogs. Many school gyms and sports training centers have the *Super Vertical Leaper* on site, so there may be no need to purchase this expensive piece of equipment.

Training Surface

Plyometric training can be executed on any *reasonably* soft surface. Rubberized running tracks, specialized plyometric flooring, and low-cut grass are best. Wood gym floors are acceptable, albeit a little harder on the body. Engaging in plyometrics on hard surfaces such as pavement or on uneven terrain should be avoided.

Footwear

Because the large majority of plyometric exercises are of the high-impact variety, it is essential that you wear *proper footwear* during your training sessions. This will lessen the chance of injury and ensure peak performance. What you wear on the volleyball court is suggested, as this type of footwear provides lateral support, is sufficiently cushioned, and has nonslip soles. Running or jogging shoes lack lateral stability and leave you susceptible to twisted knees and ankles. As such, they should be avoided for plyometric training. Performing plyometrics barefoot is also not recommended.

Schedule Description

Program Length

The *length* of a plyometric training program will vary depending upon the dynamics of your season. (High school, college, and junior high campaigns all have different time spans.) Most programs will last between 12 and 14 weeks, beginning in the mid off-season after a base of strength and conditioning has been achieved and culminating a week to 10 days prior to the commencement of regular season practice. As discussed throughout this section, plyometrics is very demanding, so attempting to employ this training method on a year-round basis is not recommended.

Number of Workouts Per Week

Because of the demanding nature of plyometric training, no more than two workouts per week should be scheduled. The individual sessions should be separated by a minimum of 48 hours and preferably 72 hours.

Sets and Repetitions

As with strength training, sets and repetitions will *vary* with the athletes needs, level of strength and fitness, experience with plyometrics, and time of year. Typically, a total of 100 to 200 contacts (repetitions) per workout should occur. For best results, spread the repetitions among three to four different plyometric drills. Three to six sets per exercise are recommended. The repetition range per set will usually be between 6 and 12.

Rest Between Sets

The level of intensity at which you are training mostly determines the rest periods between sets of plyometric exercises. For warm-up movements and low-intensity work, one minute or so between sets should be sufficient. High-intensity efforts on the other hand can take up to three minutes to recover from. Once you've become familiar with your own personal ability and level of conditioning, planning rest intervals for plyometric exercises will be relatively easy.

Workout Duration

Plyometric workouts should generally range between 20 and 40 minutes. Again, much depends on your level of strength, conditioning, and your age. Engaging in plyometric training sessions over 40 minutes is not recommended regardless of athletic ability.

In-Season Plyometrics

Because of the grueling nature of the competitive volleyball season, plyometric training should be used *sparingly* if at all during the regular season. The only exceptions would be for players not receiving much playing time or if the schedule allows for a prolonged break.

Keys to Safe and Productive Plyometric Training

Preparation

Proper preparation is without question the most important factor to successful, injury-free plyometric training. Engaging in these demanding workouts without a solid strength and conditioning base is a recipe for disaster, and will likely lead to frustration and injury.

Athletes must have a minimum of 10 to 12 weeks of weight-room strength training behind them prior to embarking on a plyometrics program. Lower-body strength work is most important. Conventional guidelines suggest that athletes should be able to leg press 2.5 times their body weight and/or squat 1.5 to 2 times their body weight before commencing with intense plyometric workouts. Keep in mind that these are just averages and attaining the previous strength-to-body-weight ratios is not a prerequisite for all. That said, it is still important to achieve a solid base of strength, conditioning, and flexibility before starting with your plyometric training program.

Learn Proper Execution

Performing plyometric drills correctly is essential to safe and effective workouts. The high-intensity and high-impact nature of plyometrics requires you to *pay close attention* to execution or risk injury. For best and safe results, perform your first few training sessions at half speed, focusing on technique and form, rather than velocity and intensity. It is also advisable to seek out an experienced sports training specialist to help guide you through your beginning plyometric workouts.

Warm Up and Cool Down Properly

Plyometric training, similar to all conditioning disciplines, requires a *full* warm-up and cool-down. Refer to Chapter 1 for a detailed explanation of warm-up and cool-down techniques.

Progression

Once proper technique is mastered, you should progress from the simpler plyometric movements to the more *complicated variety*. Intensity levels should be ramped up as well. Similar to strength training, *progression* is the name of the game with plyometrics.

Effort and Intensity

Plyometric drills are designed to be executed at a *high level* of intensity. Once your warm-up sets are concluded, it is imperative that every movement in your workout be performed with all-out effort.

Be Creative

Although the drills detailed at the conclusion of this chapter are a good start, they provide only a sampling of the many plyometric exercises available to you. You have virtually hundreds of plyometric drills from which to choose. Once you learn the basics of plyometric training, you are encouraged to experiment with different exercises. Many young athletes even design there own plyometric movements, so feel free to do that as well. This *creative approach* will make your training more interesting and ultimately more successful.

Who Should Not Engage In Plyometrics

While plyometric exercise is recommended for most improvement-conscious volleyball players, certain individuals should avoid this type of training. The following three scenarios illustrate instances where athletes should not engage in plyometrics.

- *Pre-adolescents*: Pre-adolescent athletes, even if physically mature for their age, should refrain from using plyometrics. The risk of injury to muscles, bones, and joints is substantially higher prior to puberty than it is afterward. Young athletes would be better served using there time and energy perfecting volleyball skills and for general strength and conditioning rather than pushing the envelope experimenting with advanced, high-impact training methods like plyometrics.

- *Injured athletes*: Injured athletes or athletes with a history of lower-body injuries should abstain from plyometrics. This may seem obvious, but believe it or not through the years many trainers have encountered numerous misguided athletes engaging plyometric training while injured or during injury rehabilitation. Injuries and plyometrics don't mix. Unless, of course, your goal is to worsen your injured condition.

- *Large athletes*: Large athletes (i.e., those individuals weighing more than 225 pounds or so) must take great care with plyometrics. Some may opt to skip this particular conditioning discipline altogether. The force of most landings during plyometric drills is high, and larger volleyball players are much more susceptible to injury than their smaller counterparts. Many bigger athletes should choose simpler exercises such as net jumps, cone hops, or double-leg jumps in their plyometric training to decrease the wear and tear while still getting some benefit. Of course this is an individual matter and all athletes big and small must judge their own individual tolerance for plyometrics.

Don't Overdo It

Just to re-emphasize, plyometrics is an *extremely demanding* form of athletic conditioning. Too much plyometric work can cause overtraining and body breakdown in short order for even the most gifted of athletes. Volleyball players are especially susceptible to plyometrics-induced overtraining, since the game itself entails so much jumping and landing. Work hard during your plyometric sessions, just keep things in perspective and take care not to overdo it. By approaching training in this manner you will not be disappointed (or injured).

Beginner Plyometric Drills

Drill: Net Touches

Execution: Facing a volleyball net or other elevated object such as a basketball rim or football goalpost, assume an erect and balanced stance, with your head up and your eyes fixed at the top of the net. Proceed by bending quickly to the jumping position (approximately three-quarter to parallel) and instantaneously explode upward toward the target, reaching up with one hand as high as possible over the net. Repeat for the required repetitions, always focusing on popping off the floor as quickly as possible.

Drill: Double-Leg Jumps

Execution: Assume an erect and balanced stance with your head straight and your eyes focused in front of you. Continue by bending quickly into the jumping position and immediately explode straight up in the air as high as possible, while concurrently pulling your knees up toward your chest. During the jump phase of the drill, your arms should be straight out in front of you. Similar to net touches, the idea is to pop off the ground quickly upon landing and to rise up as high as you can on each jump.

Drill: Front Cone/Barrier Hops

Execution: Place a small cone/barrier (approximately 6 to 12 inches in height) directly in front of you. With your feet shoulder-width apart and your knees flexed, broad jump over the cone/barrier, concentrating on jumping as high as possible. During the airborne phase of the drill your body should be in a straight line. After you've landed, turn 180 degrees, and repeat the jump. Continue for the required number of repetitions.

Drill: Overhead Toss

Execution: Stand with your knees slightly flexed and your feet close together, holding an appropriately weighted medicine ball overhead. Step forward explosively and release the ball powerfully when it reaches head height. Repeat for the required number of repetitions. This drill is best performed with a partner of the same athletic ability and strength.

Intermediate Plyometric Drills

Drill: Side Cone/Barrier Jumps

Execution: Line up four to six cones/barriers, spaced two- to four-feet apart. The height of the cones/barriers will vary from six inches to one foot. Stand sideways at the end of the line of cones/barriers with your feet at shoulder width and your knees flexed. Proceed to jump laterally over the row of cones/barriers. When you clear the last cone/barrier, land on your outside foot and drive off it immediately and powerfully to change direction. Continue to land two-footed until clearing the final cone/barrier on the other side of the line and repeat.

Drill: Alternating Box Push-Offs

Execution: Stand with one foot placed on a 6- to 12-inch box or stair, with your other foot planted firmly on the ground. Push off powerfully with your raised leg and jump straight up as high as possible. Reverse your legs in the air and land with the opposite leg on the box. Repeat in quick fashion for the required number of repetitions. Swing both arms upward in unison during the jump phase. This will add height and control.

Drill: Backward Toss

Execution: Stand with your knees bent and your feet slightly wider than shoulder width and pick up an appropriately weight medicine ball from the ground. Proceed to swing the ball between your legs, and as your forearms come just short of your thighs, reverse direction and throw the ball up over your head as far as possible. Repeat for the required number of repetitions. As with all medicine ball throwing exercises, it is suggested that you perform this drill with a partner of equal athletic ability and strength.

Drill: Power Skips

Execution: Starting in a slow jog, gradually begin running, exaggerating your arm swing and knee lift. Your upper leg of the driving knee should be slightly above parallel to the running surface. Attempt to cover as much distance as possible during the airborne phase of the movement. As with all plyometric running and jumping exercises, try to spend as little time as possible in contact with the ground.

Advanced Plyometric Drills

Drill: Front Single-Box Jumps With Step Down

Execution: Stand facing a box, with your knees flexed, your feet shoulder-width apart, and your hands at your sides. The height of the box should vary from one to three feet, depending on your athletic ability. Jump on to the box, landing under control on two feet. Pause briefly, then step off the box with one foot, drop to the floor, and immediately spring off two feet as high as possible straight into the air (one repetition). Repeat for the required number of repetitions.

Drill: Front Multiple-Box Jumps

Execution: Line up three to five boxes, approximately three- to five-feet apart. The height of the boxes should vary from one to three feet, depending on your athletic ability. Face the line of boxes as you maintain an athletic stance (knees flexed, feet at shoulder width, and hands at your sides). Proceed to jump on and off each box in succession, landing on the ground between each box, and concentrating on spending as little time out of the air as possible. Deliberately walk back to the front of the line and repeat for the required number of repetitions.

Drill: Plyometric Push-Ups

Execution: With your feet raised behind you on a box or a step, assume a conventional push-up position. The box/step can range from six inches to two feet in height depending on your size and athletic ability. Begin by pushing up explosively, allowing your hands to leave the ground. When your hands return to the ground, catch yourself and immediately explode upward for another repetition. Repeat for the required number of repetitions.

Drill: Medicine Ball Squat Jump

Execution: Begin by assuming a shoulder-width stance, with your feet pointed slightly outward. Take hold of an appropriately weighted medicine ball and place it behind your neck. Proceed to squat down parallel to the floor or just below, and explode upward, jumping straight up as high as you can while keeping the resistance (medicine ball) in contact with your neck and shoulders throughout. Repeat for the required number of repetitions.

CHAPTER 11

Speed, Quickness, and Agility

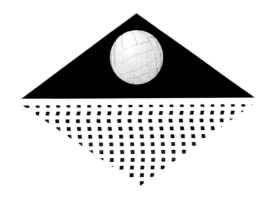

Speed Training

For decades a well-established myth circulated around the sports training world that it was impossible for athletes to increase sprinting speed. "Sprinters were born, not made," was the popular saying of the day even among longtime track coaches.

Thankfully, this well-entrenched belief has finally been put to rest, as numerous athletes in a variety of sports routinely show speed improvements from year to year, the result of hard work, dedication, and proper training. Speed training is no longer the exclusive bastion of world-class sprinters. All athletes *can* learn and train to run faster.

While straight-ahead speed is not as important as explosive quickness and vertical jumping ability to the volleyball players, over the course of a match athletes are required to sprint 20, 30, even 40 feet to retrieve a ball. Therefore, learning proper running technique, and engaging in various speed-enhancing drills is worthwhile for all volleyball players.

Keys to Efficient Sprinting

Conditioning

The first step toward reaching your speed potential is attaining good overall *physical condition*. Without going into detail here (the rest of the book does that), this process includes developing a solid strength base, especially in the lower body, establishing satisfactory aerobic and anaerobic fitness, maintaining optimal body composition—excess body fat will obviously slow you down—and achieving a high level of flexibility. One look at world-class sprinters and you'll quickly notice all are in great shape with powerfully built physiques and extremely low levels of body fat, ripped if you will.

Running Mechanics

The most important variable in increasing sprinting speed involves improving your *running mechanics*. Although every individual athlete has a unique running style, you can choose from many fundamental sprint-enhancing practices that will help you get the most out of your natural ability.

With regard to running mechanics, the two major factors in how fast you run can be described by a simple equation: *stride length* x *stride frequency* = *sprinting speed*. Stride length is the space covered in an individual stride. Stride frequency is the time it takes to accomplish a single stride. To become a faster sprinter, you must enhance your stride length by intensifying your force against the track or court, while maintaining balance with your stride frequency. Powerful and efficient arm movement also must be employed. The following list details the characteristics of efficient sprinting:

- Running in a naturally erect position is central to good sprinting technique. Many young athletes have been erroneously taught to lean forward when sprinting. This positioning will actually slow you down and can contribute to a loss of balance at high speeds.

- Your head should be up and straight, with your eyes focused toward the destination of the sprint.

- Your arms, shoulders, and hands should be relaxed when sprinting. Many athletes have a tendency to keep their torsos rigid when running at top speed. Remember, to reach your sprinting potential, you must always remain relaxed.

- Your push-off leg should always end up completely extended, and it is important not to overstride during your stride cycle. Increasing your stride length in an unnatural fashion by forcing your lead foot to land far ahead of your body will hinder your sprinting speed.

- Your arm action should come from your shoulders. During the upswing, your hands should reach just in front of your chin and slightly inside your shoulders. On the downswing, your hands should reach no further back than your hips.

- Artificially increasing your stride frequency by attempting to move your legs too quickly will make you move fast but mostly in one place—not very helpful when it comes to chasing down a volleyball. Traversing the maximum amount of ground in the shortest period of time involves the correct balance of stride length and stride frequency.

- Your elbows should always be kept at a 90-degree angle, forcing all the arm action to stay close to your body. If your arms are too far from your torso when sprinting, it will more times than not disrupt your stride rhythm.

- Your torso should remain mostly stationary when sprinting, and the shoulders must be squared to your destination.

Like any other athletic skill, sprinting properly requires *repetitive practice*. Try to follow the previous guidelines during your anaerobic conditioning workouts and when performing volleyball specific drills that entail sprinting. If you have the opportunity, seek out an experienced track coach to help you perfect your running form. Most high school and all college programs have experienced track coaches on staff who are usually more than happy to share their expertise. Some athletes may go as far as hiring a running coach. If you decide to go the (expensive) route, just make sure the trainer's credentials are legitimate.

Training Methods to Increase Speed

Other than improving your running form and attaining optimal physical condition and body weight, a variety of speed-enhancing methods are at you disposal. A few of the most popular are detailed in the following examples.

Acceleration Sprints

Acceleration sprints involve *gradually increasing* your speed during the course of a run. For example, if you were engaging in a 100-meter acceleration sprint, you would begin by jogging about 15 meters, accelerate to a stride for 30 meters or so, and then proceed to an all-out sprint for approximately 55 meters. Between sprints, walk 50 to 60 meters, and then repeat the sequence. Acceleration sprints will help you improve your running form, while at the same time providing a high-level speed workout.

Added Resistance Sprinting

As the name suggests, added resistance sprinting calls for *adding weight or resistance* to your frame to make the act of sprinting more difficult. You can accomplish this in a number of ways. The following are some documented favorites:

- *Weighted-vest sprinting*: Weighted vests are used in a variety of volleyball training disciplines, including plyometrics and sand jumping, both of which are detailed in this book. Sprinting while wearing a weighted vest has shown to be an effective way to increase running speed. However, you must follow certain safety parameters.

  First, the weight of the vest should never be heavier than 8 to 10 percent of your body weight. A higher ratio of vest weight to body weight will increase your chance of injury substantially

  Second, weight should be added to the vest gradually as strength, conditioning, and speed improves. Even elite athletes engage in a minimum of half-a-dozen weighted-vest sprint workouts before the aforementioned vest-weight-to-body-weight ratio is achieved.

  Third, it is imperative that proper and natural running form be maintained at all times during weighted-vest sprint workouts. If the weight of the vest interferes with your running technique guess what—the vest is too heavy. It is always better to perform these training sessions with less weight, rather than compromising form and risking injury by pushing it.

  Finally, if you suffer from lower-back or knee problems, running with a weighted vest is not recommended. The additional weight, even if it is only a small percentage of your body weight, can easily exacerbate previous conditions.

- *Two-person harness*: The two-person harness is used frequently by track athletes and football players. Training with the two-person harness entails having one partner hold the handles tightly without giving ground while the other partner sprints straight ahead at full speed pulling the resistance. It helps if your partner is approximately the same weight as you for obvious reasons.

- *Water sprinting*: As mentioned elsewhere in this book, water workouts have become extremely popular in the sports training world. For sprinting purposes, water provides natural resistance, thus running in a pool is great low-impact way to improve speed. Water treadmills are available at many health clubs and fitness centers. This equipment allows you to run on a submerged footpad against water current resistance that can be adjusted to fit your needs. Needless to say, this is a tremendous speed and conditioning training tool for injured athletes who are not yet ready for ground pounding.

- *Medicine ball ladder high-knee sprints*: While the name of this speed enhancing technique is a mouth full, it is actually quite a simple drill. Two pieces of equipment are required: an appropriately weighted medicine ball and a speed ladder. The ladder is made of nylon and has rungs that gradually increase in length. Speed ladders are adjustable and usually stretch to about 15 yards.

  Before beginning, lay out the ladder on a running track or another even, semi-soft terrain. Start at the end of the ladder where the rungs are closest together and hold a medicine ball directly overhead. Proceed to move through the ladder with high-knee action, concentrating on making quick, powerful foot strikes. Repeat for the required number of repetitions. To increase the level of difficulty, try performing medicine ball ladder high-knee sprints in soft sand.

- *Resistance bands, parachutes, and sleds*: These pieces of equipment basically simulate the two-person harness training effect. The only difference is that a partner is not required. Bands can be affixed to any solid object, parachutes open with a hand release, and sleds connect to the sprinter by a torso harness. These apparatuses all have their flaws, however. Bands are known to break during a run, parachutes have a tendency not to open, and sleds can be awkward to use, especially if the running surface you're training on is not neatly manicured. Therefore if you have a choice, the two-person harness should be the pick.

Overspeed Training

Overspeed training *improves* sprinting speed by increasing your stride length and rate. Similar to plyometrics, this type of workout forces your neuromuscular system to become accustomed to faster speeds, and therefore enables you to attain those speeds without facilitation.

- *Downhill sprinting*: The most popular form of overspeed training is downhill sprinting. It requires no fancy equipment, and if you can locate a hill with the appropriate decline angle, you're all set. Finding the proper running area is the real challenge though. Generally, you should try to pinpoint a 40-meter or so stretch that has an approximate three-degree downgrade. Anything steeper is not advisable, because it will cause you to compromise running form and may be dangerous. Downhill sprints that cover 20 to 30 meters work best for volleyball players. As with all forms of sprinting, a thorough warm-up and cool-down should always be performed.

- *Towing*: Towing is perhaps the most efficient form of overspeed training available. Many athletes in a variety of sports have lowered sprint times substantially by incorporating this method. The downside to towing is that most individuals and schools do not have access to the necessary equipment for this form of training, such as elastic tubing. Also, because of the intense and complicated nature of this technique, capable oversight by an experienced track coach or athletic conditioning specialist is a must for all workouts.

Towing workouts should always take place on a soft, even grassy surface, such as a football or soccer field. Soft terrain is a must for these sessions, as spills are commonplace. The towing apparatus is made of elastic tubing and should measure 20 to 25 feet. It will be attached to your waist by a belt, while the other end will be secured to a partner or secure object like a football goalpost. After a few warm-up strides, walk backward about 30 meters from where the tubing is attached and proceed to sprint all-out as the tubing snaps back and pulls you forward. It is very important that proper running form is maintained during all towing sprints. Also, avoid stretching the tubing too far. Most well-made elastic tubing will stretch five to six times its relaxed length. For safety reasons, check the tubing carefully for any damage prior to all training sessions.

Quickness and Agility Training

Quickness and agility are ever-present in volleyball. The game has become extremely fast-paced at all levels of play and most movements on the volleyball court require split-second timing and cat-quick reactions. If you're not ahead of the play, you're behind it. So whether you're reacting to a hard-driven ball or positioning yourself for a point-saving block you have very little room for error. Needless to say, volleyball players should make *improving* their quickness and agility a priority.

More so than straight-ahead speed, quickness and agility can be increased significantly. Many athletes, including numerous volleyball players, have become substantially quicker and more agile after a year of dedicated and focused work. Following the quickness/agility program prescribed in the next section will ensure that you reach your full quickness and agility potential.

Schedule Description

Similar to your plyometric program, the quickness/agility schedule will cover 12 to 14 weeks, beginning in the mid off-season and ending a week or so before the start of organized practice sessions. Before embarking on a quickness/agility program, it is *essential* that you have developed a solid base of strength and aerobic/anaerobic conditioning. This is accomplished by following the strength and conditioning recommendations presented earlier in the book. The quickness/agility workouts themselves should take place two days per week and are best executed immediately following your plyometric drills. (Plyometrics and quickness/agility training have much in common.) During the regular volleyball season, because team practices will provide sufficient agility-related exercise, specific quickness/agility workouts are usually not necessary. The only exceptions being if your not receiving much playing time or are coming back after an injury or some other extended lay-off.

Quickness/agility sessions are best performed on a volleyball/basketball court. While other soft surfaces such as rubberized running tracks or manicured grass fields are adequate, volleyball/basketball courts provide floor lines that can be conveniently used as markers. All quickness/agility drills should be undertaken at full speed, unless otherwise specified. The goal is to get your body, more specifically your feet, in the habit of moving quickly on demand. This is achieved by going *all-out* during every exercise with the emphasis on spending as little time as possible in one place. The emphasis is always on high-intensity execution. Table 11-1 presents an overview of the basic parameters for conducting quickness/agility training.

Quickness/Agility Drills

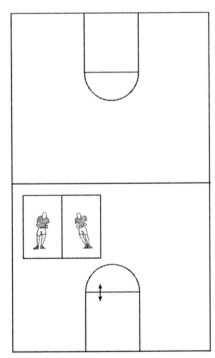 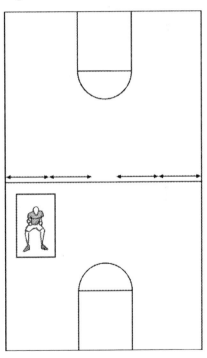

Drill: Quick Feet

Drill: Side Shuffle

Execution: Stand parallel to the end line or sideline with your feet close together. On command, hop back and forth over the line as fast as possible. Continue for the required time.

Execution: Start in an athletic ready stance. With your knees flexed and your back taut, proceed to side shuffle back and forth across the width of the court for the required time.

Program length: 12 to 14 weeks	
Drill duration: 15 to 30 seconds	
Drills per workout: 3 to 4	
Rest intervals: 30 to 60 seconds	
Sets: 6 to 8	
Intensity: Very high	

Table 11-1. Recommended parameters for quickness/agility training

Drill: Side Shuffle with Response

Execution: Start in an athletic ready stance. Have a partner shout *move*, and proceed to side shuffle right or left. When your partner shouts move again, change direction quickly and side shuffle the opposite way. Continue to side shuffle back and forth on response for the required time.

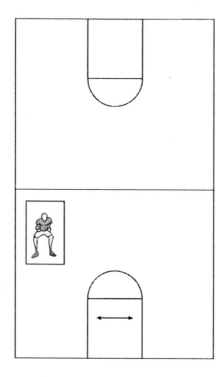

Drill: Beanbag Pass and Catch

Execution: Stand facing a partner six to eight feet apart, each holding a small beanbag in one hand. (A squash or tennis ball may be substituted for the beanbag.) Side shuffle across the court while softly tossing the balls back and forth. As you become proficient at the drill, begin to incorporate more difficult throws (in front, behind, high, low, etc.) to your partner. Continue for required time.

Drill: Mini-Cone Shuffle

Execution: Place a series of mini-cones or other low-lying barriers a foot or so apart. Using small side steps, shuffle over the cones without crossing your feet and concentrating on spending as little time as possible on the ground. When you get to the end of the row, reverse course and repeat back and forth for the required time.

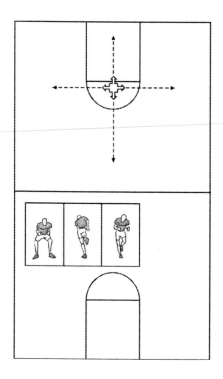

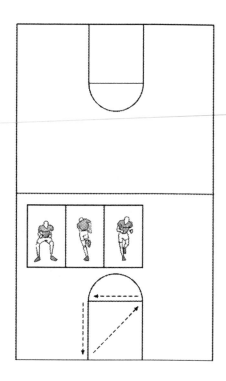

Drill: Change Direction with Response

Execution: Assume an athletic stance. Have your partner stand facing you at approximately 15 feet. Respond to your partner's direction to either side—shuffle left or right, backpedal, or sprint straight ahead. Continue for the required time.

Drill: Sprint, Slide, Backpedal

Execution: Assume an athletic stance where the basketball lane line intersects the baseline (on either side). On command, sprint diagonally across the basketball three-second area to where the opposite lane line meets the basketball foul line. Then, immediately side shuffle across the foul line to the opposite lane line. From there, proceed without pausing to backpedal to the starting position. Continue in this pattern for the required time. Alternate starting sides for each set.

Drill: Reaction Belt Response Drill

Execution: To start, both you and your partner will fasten a five-foot, Velcro reaction belt to your waists. Your partner will then proceed in no set pattern to make a series of quick movements and you should attempt to follow as closely as possible. The objective is to keep the belt on as long as you can without it breaking free, preferably for the duration of the drill. To get the most out of the drill, try to engage a partner who is quicker and more agile than you.

Drill: Reaction Ball Chase

Execution: Assume an athletic stance facing your partner. Then, have your partner drop or throw a reaction ball (a small ridged ball that bounces in unpredictable directions) five to eight feet in front of you. Proceed to chase the ball down, pick it up, and return it to your partner. Repeat for the required number of repetitions or time.

CHAPTER 12

Cross Training Options

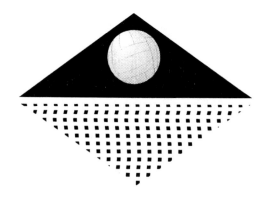

While the training choices in this book are certainly sufficient to keep even the most advanced volleyball player in top-flight condition, it wouldn't be complete if it didn't include some *cross training options*. Cross training periodically will keep your workouts interesting, help prevent overuse injuries, and assist in heading off fitness plateaus that might otherwise arise. This chapter reviews seven different training modalities volleyball players may want to consider incorporating into their year-round conditioning program.

Basketball

Basketball players are universally recognized as the *most* athletic and highly conditioned athletes in all of sport. They posses a combination speed, strength, quickness, and jumping ability that is unparalleled among team sport participants. In fact, many top basketball players, if trained properly, would have great success on the volleyball court.

Playing basketball regularly in the off-season will provide numerous benefits for volleyball players. First, from a conditioning standpoint, basketball is perhaps the best *outside activity* a volleyball player can engage in. It exercises all three energy systems (aerobic, lactic acid, and ATP-PC), and the physical-contact aspect of the game increases the conditioning effect, not to mention an athlete's toughness.

Second, basketball's *movement patterns* are very similar to volleyball, with jumping, running, sliding, and backpedaling all occurring frequently. Basketball forces athletes to respond to situations at a moment's notice (avoiding a screen, alluding a defender, guarding a quick-footed ball handler, etc.). This will enhance your ability to *anticipate and react*, two extremely important skills for volleyball players to develop.

Finally, playing basketball will give you a break from the game of volleyball, while still providing conditioning and athleticism benefits. All athletes can get burned out from engaging in the same activity week after week and month after month. Volleyball players are no exception. So enjoying a game of basketball from time to time will keep your mind clear and your body fresh.

One word of caution before this section is concluded: playing basketball outdoors on concrete courts can take its toll on your body, and is therefore not recommended for volleyball players. Do your knees, shins, and lower back a favor—keep your basketball participation to wood flooring.

Jumping Rope

Every volleyball player should own a *jump rope*. In fact, every volleyball player should own three jump ropes; a light-handled, easy-turning rope; a heavy-handled rope; and a heavy-corded rope. Working out regularly with a variety of jump ropes will help improve many aspects of your volleyball conditioning and athleticism. Training with an easy-turning rope will help enhance your quickness, footwork, hand speed, and coordination. It is also a great tool for improving your aerobic conditioning, as the rope's easy-turning feature will allow you to jump for extended periods of time without tiring. Jumping with a heavy-handled rope will improve your hand, wrist, and forearm strength, along with providing a terrific workout for your anaerobic lactic acid system. Exercising with a heavy-corded rope is great for stimulating your anaerobic ATP-PC system, and will aid in building strength throughout your upper body, especially your shoulders. Working out with this high-resistance rope will augment your ability to move quickly and explosively on the volleyball court.

Jumping rope is *highly recommended* for all volleyball players, but the benefits are especially pertinent to taller, younger athletes, many of whom have slow feet, poor footwork, and lack overall coordination. Skipping regularly forces big players to make a habit of moving their feet quickly and consistently. It also provides a coordination-enhancing training vehicle that can help them to gain confidence in their ever-growing bodies.

Tips for Effective Jump Rope Workouts

- *Rope length*: A jump rope should be long enough to reach armpit to armpit, while passing under both feet. Some volleyball players, because of their height and long limbs, may have difficulty finding a long enough rope at retail outlets. In that case, try contacting a few jump rope manufacturers or scanning fitness product catalogs or companies online. Some manufacturers may actually be able to custom design a rope for you.

- *Turning the jump rope*: Turning the jump rope is a fairly simple process. It entails turning your hands and wrists in a natural forward circle. Your upper arms should be held close to your torso, and your forearms should be pointed downward at a 45-degree angle. Your wrists and hands do most of the work when turning a light-handled rope; your forearms come into play when turning a heavy-handled rope; and your shoulder girdle is engaged when turning a heavy-corded rope.

- *Where to jump*: It is best to conduct your rope-jumping workouts on semi-soft surfaces—wood volleyball courts and rubberized running tracks are ideal. You can find specialized pads for rope jumping at most sporting goods stores, which can be used both indoors and outdoors. Hard surfaces, such as concrete and asphalt, should be avoided when jumping rope.

- *Warm up lower legs thoroughly*: Jumping rope can be extremely taxing on the lower legs (calves, shins, and ankles). To prevent injury and post-workout soreness, it is imperative that you warm up and stretch your lower legs thoroughly prior to a rope-jumping session.

- *Jumping patterns*: Although you have virtually hundreds of jumping patterns to choose from when jumping rope, the following three basic methods are all you need to enjoy productive workouts:

  - *Alternate foot jump*: The athlete jumps once each rope turn, alternating between his left and right foot. Jumping in this manner resembles running in place.

  - *Two-foot jump*: The athlete jumps once each rope turn, with both feet hitting the ground simultaneously. Your feet should be slightly closer than shoulder-width when executing this jumping pattern

  - *Skip jump*: The athlete jumps once each rope turn, alternating in no set sequence between left foot, right foot, and both feet simultaneously.

  Once you master these jump rope techniques, you are encouraged to learn more complicated jumping patterns as you see fit, especially if jumping rope becomes a large part of your conditioning program.

Boxing

What does boxing have to do with volleyball you ask? Well, not much in a literal sense. However, certain aspects of boxing training will enhance both your volleyball workouts and on-court performance. It takes as little as a half-dozen boxing lessons to become proficient enough to have productive training sessions, and most volleyball players, because of the nature of their sport, adjust fairly easily to boxing. Boxing workouts involve shadow boxing, footwork drills, rope skipping, abdominal training, medicine ball work, hitting the heavy bags and speed bags, and ring work with an experienced trainer. Live sparring is not necessary nor is it recommended for volleyball players.

The benefits of regular boxing training include the following: heavy-bag work will loosen and strengthen all the muscles of the upper body; footwork will be improved by skipping rope and by performing in-ring sliding drills; hand-eye coordination will be enhanced by working the speed bag and by shadow boxing; and medicine ball and abdominal training will strengthen and condition the core of your body. A boxing workout also provides both anaerobic and aerobic conditioning benefits. It is highly recommended that you search out a boxing gym in your area and sign up for some lessons. If you do not have a conventional boxing gym near you, many commercial health clubs today offer boxing instruction. So try your hand at the *sweet science* as boxing has been called, and take advantage of superb conditioning tool. Table 12-1 presents a sample boxing workout.

1 round shadow boxing (warm-up)	2 rounds footwork drills
1 round rope skipping	2 rounds rope skipping
3 rounds heavy bag	2 rounds abdominal work
2 rounds speed bag	1 round shadow boxing (cool-down)

- The workout is based on three-minute rounds and one-minute rest intervals between rounds.
- Total workout time = 57 minutes

Table 12-1. Sample boxing workout

Weighted-Vest Sand Jumping

Perhaps more so than any of the cross training options discussed in this chapter, weighted-vest sand jumping is tailor made for volleyball players. The combination of added resistance from the vest and the fact that you're jumping off soft sand provides a *potent and intense* jump workout, one that if engaged in regularly, will produce substantial improvements in your vertical jump.

The benefits of performing these explosive jumps are not limited to improving jumping ability, however. It also affords a tremendous anaerobic conditioning workout, exercising both the ATP-PC and lactic acid systems to their fullest. In fact, weighted-vest sand jumping can periodically take the place of any of the exercise modalities detailed in the anaerobic training section in Chapter 5. And to top it off, this form of training is very safe, as the sand provides an extremely soft and forgiving surface on which to land, and that is especially important when extra resistance is employed.

The number of sets and repetitions you perform during your weighted-vest sand workouts will have much to do with your physical condition. But four to six sets of 15 to 25 jumps per set is the usual range for most competitive volleyball players.

Before beginning your sand workout, especially if you're performing it on a public beach, carefully check the terrain for broken glass, rocks, sharp seashells, or any other object that has the potential to cause injury. Unfortunately, beaches these days are used for much more than just volleyball, sunning, and swimming.

Uphill Sprinting

While you do have a choice of numerous resistance-sprinting techniques—many that make use of fancy equipment such as parachutes, sleds, and bands—keep in mind an old standby that is simple, costs you nothing in terms of equipment, and most important, actually works. This standby is called *uphill sprinting,* a tried and true method that increases running speed, explosiveness, and anaerobic conditioning.

Uphill sprinting is highly popular with track athletes (mostly short-distance sprinters) and football players. In fact, ageless wide receiver Jerry Rice, perhaps the greatest football player in the history of the NFL, swears by it. (Rice spends many hours each off-season running up hills readying himself for preseason training camp.) Most volleyball players probably have not been exposed to uphill sprinting, since straight-ahead running speed is not coveted in the sport. It is nevertheless a proven technique that should be incorporated at least periodically in all explosive-sport athletes training regimes.

The hill grade you use during uphill sprint workouts will vary depending upon availability of the appropriate landscape. But, as a rule, steep grades (7 to 10-degree angles) should be utilized for short, explosive sprints, covering 10 to 15 yards or so. Flatter grades (1.5 to 3.5- degree angles) should be used for sprints ranging from 20 to 80 yards. A weighted vest or any other form of added resistance should not be incorporated during uphill sprints. The hills themselves will provide all the resistance you need to achieve productive workouts.

Medicine Ball Slides

Medicine ball slides strengthens both the upper and lower body in unison, provides a solid anaerobic workout, helps to improve footwork, and engenders mental toughness. The execution is simple. Hold an appropriately weighted medicine ball at chest height with your arms approximately 85-percent extended. Proceed to slide without crossing your feet and, while keeping the ball stationary for 10 to 12 yards in one direction, change direction and slide back to the starting position. How many times you slide back and forth depends on your level of conditioning and strength. Most competitive volleyball players should be able to do three to four up-and-backs without stopping (one set) for three to five sets.

If you have the luxury of a partner, slides can be performed while passing the medicine ball back and forth over the 10- to 12-yard course. This adds a degree of concentration, along with helping to improve your hand-eye coordination.

Failure Sprinting

Failure sprinting is far and away the most *exhausting* form of cross training discussed in this chapter. This technique is not well known nor widely prescribed in the sports-conditioning community—probably because it is so painful to perform. Failure sprinting, as the name insinuates, entails running at full speed for as long as your body holds up—no breaks, no let ups, just sprinting until you can't sprint anymore. The distance you cover will depend on your speed, physical conditioning, and your ability to handle discomfort. As you can imagine, this technique of conditioning should only be engaged in by athletes who are in *top shape*.

Failure sprints are best performed on a long, flat straightaway. If a straightaway is not available, sprinting to failure on a track or even back and forth on a volleyball court will do. It is recommended that you begin each failure sprint with 20 to 30 yards of striding to gradually pick up speed. The rest intervals between sets should correlate with the work:ratios detailed in Chapter 5. Three to five failure sprints per workout are suggested for competitive, highly conditioned volleyball players. Again, only try this cross training option if you are in *excellent* physical condition.

ABOUT THE AUTHOR

Tom Emma is the president of Power Performance, Inc., a company that specializes in training athletes in strength, conditioning, and athletic-enhancement techniques. He is a graduate of Duke University, where he was a three-year starter on the basketball team and squad captain his senior year. His .843 career free-throw percentage is among the highest in Duke history. He was drafted by the Chicago Bulls in the 1983 NBA draft. Tom has a masters degree from Columbia University and lives in New York City. His first book, *Peak Performance Training for Basketball*, was also published by Coaches Choice.